ALSO BY FRANK McCLAIN

Job Hunting Ninja Master 2017

The multi-award-winning ***Job Hunting Ninja Master 2017*** won the **Foreword Reviews'** prestigious **2016** *Foreword INDIES Book of the Year Award.* In a competition with over 1500 other entrants whose books were judged by a panel of over 150 judges made up of librarians and booksellers reading every page, the judges chose ***Job Hunting Ninja Master 2017*** as the **Book of the Year** for job hunters.

IT Questions & Answers For IT Job Interviews, Volume 1
General IT Knowledge, Transmission Lines and Cabling,
Voice over IP (VoIP), Video and Telepresence over IP, Wireless (WiFi)

IT Questions & Answers For IT Job Interviews, Volume 2
IPv4 and IPv6 Addressing, NAT, Layer 2 Switching Concepts,
Layer 3 Routing Concepts

IT Questions & Answers For IT Job Interviews, Volume 3
BGP Routing, EIGRP Routing, OSPF Routing

IT Questions & Answers For IT Job Interviews, Volume 4
Data Center and Virtualization, F5 Networks Load Balancer,
Riverbed WAN Optimization

IT Questions & Answers For IT Job Interviews, Volume 5
Access Lists and Prefix Lists, Tunnels and VPNs, Cisco ASA Firewall

IT Questions & Answers For IT Job Interviews, Volume 6
Service Provider Networks, Quality of Service (QoS),
Troubleshooting Router and Switch Interfaces

AWARDS FOR YOU'RE HIRED!

The award-winning *YOU'RE HIRED!* is rated "Best in Class" by winning the **Independent Book Publishers Association 2017 Benjamin Franklin Digital Award.**

"I have read 'YOU'RE HIRED' by Frank McClain and have found it a solid reference manual for the job seeker . . . rated 'Very Good' . . . there is a good section on preparation before the interview . . . exceeds user expectations very well . . . follows generally accepted principles of good writing for the genre very well . . . grammar, spelling, punctuation, etc. is very well . . . I plan on keeping this as part of my much too large collection of job hunting guides" – **IBPA Benjamin Franklin Digital Award Judge**

YOU'RE HIRED!

SUCCESS SECRETS TO PHONE & IN-PERSON JOB INTERVIEWS FOR JOB SEEKERS & CAREER CHANGERS

Frank McClain

Publisher's Note. This publication is designed to provide accurate and authoritative information in regard to the subject matter. It is sold with the understanding that the publisher is not engaged in rendering professional career, legal, financial, psychological or health services. If expert assistance is required, the service of the appropriate professional should be sought.

Edited by Clarence Z. Seacrest

Cover design by Prodesignsx

Facebook Page: http://bit.ly/2g7KHou

ISBN 978-0-9982384-6-3 (paperback)
ISBN 978-0-9982384-7-0 (ebook)

A Message To My Readers

I chose to publish this book without Digital Rights Management (DRM). Although DRM may help limit copying and pirating of digital material, it also limits the flexibility for paying readers to enjoy their ebooks on different e-reader devices of their choosing.

Although I agree with other authors that piracy of copyrighted material is wrong, I will not punish my readers by implementing DRM on my books. Therefore, you can be assured when you purchase this book in ebook format, you will be able to read it anywhere, anytime, on any of your e-reader devices.

To God be the glory.

Table of Contents

Introduction

If you're in search of a job because you quit your job, were laid off, are changing careers, a first-time job seeker, recent grad, transitioning military veteran, someone who's returning to the workforce after a long absence or employed but looking for your next dream job; you're not alone in this journey and there's no cause for shame. You're among the ranks of **millions** of people each **month** (not each year; each month!) who are in search of a new job.

In the January 2016 *Job Openings and Labor Turnover* report by the Bureau of Labor Statistics (BLS), 2.8 million Americans quit their jobs across US government and private sectors over that single month of January. In April 2016, 2.8 million Americans quit their jobs; and in July 2016, 3 million Americans quit their jobs.

This BLS report is just a sampling of the fact that people are job-searching, leaving their jobs, job-hopping and changing their careers by the droves each month of the year. These figures include only those people who voluntarily quit their jobs, not people who left their jobs through retirement or involuntarily through layoffs or being fired from their jobs. That's a lot of people. That's also a lot of competition.

Their story is your story. That's why you're reading a book about job interviews. Obviously, interviewing for a job isn't the only activity of the job search process. You have to carefully prepare your resume; there's the job search until you find the job that interests you; then there is communication that takes place between you and a company or staffing agency recruiter; you have to negotiate what hourly rate or annual salary you want for the job; and finally there's the all-important job interview.

If you're asking yourself, "Shouldn't I be reading a book about all these other job-hunting steps first before reading a book about the last step in the job search process—job interviews?" Yes, you should. If you haven't covered these other areas of the job search process that must happen before the job interview, then allow me to introduce you to my other book that covers all of these areas in great detail: *Job Hunting Ninja Master 2017.*

If you've already covered these other areas, then **YOU'RE HIRED!** is all you need to seal the deal in your next job interview.

In **YOU'RE HIRED!**, I'll cover where to locate jobs both in the US and overseas, and provide you plenty of websites where you can search for and apply for these positions. We'll look at your competition in the entire private and public sector workforces as you job-hunt and interview for jobs. I'll also cover the company and staffing agency recruiters who will most likely be ones who will set up your job interview for you.

The remainder of this book will show you how to have an Oscar-winning performance in your next job interview. This book will take you step-by-step through everything you need to know and do before, during and after the job interview process to make you stand out above all the other job-hunting candidates and get *YOU* selected for the job. The hiring manager will say to you, "**YOU'RE HIRED!**"

Let's begin your journey to your next dream job!

CHAPTER ONE

The Job Interview is a Competition

You have to learn the rules of the game.
And then you have to play better than anyone else.
Albert Einstein

So much in life is a competition. We compete for love and attention. We compete in war, in politics, in religions and philosophies. We compete in sports, in entertainment, in social media, in traffic and for the remote control. We compete with siblings while growing up. We compete in school during formal education. Then we compete for jobs throughout our working life.

Like it or not, job-hunting and job interviews are a competition. Some people are in it to win it. Some want to avoid it, but can't. Others are just spectators, watching from the sidelines. Eventually, we all have to compete at one point or another in this activity called the job interview.

Like so many other competitions, the person who masters the proper technique of the competition wins. Mastering any technique requires good coaching, good mentoring, good knowledge, good advice and good practice. Job interviews are no different. That's what led you to this book. You're searching for the knowledge that will help you be a success in the job interview process.

Many people will pay thousands of dollars for the right mentor. Attendees to a Tony Robbins seminar could pay anywhere from $650 for a general admission ticket to $2,995 for a Diamond Premiere ticket. Other people will learn from the tuition-free school of hard knocks (which oftentimes turns out to be more expensive than a Tony Robbins seminar ticket). But you've chosen the best way, the most cost effective way to learn—reading this book.

What if you could learn from someone who's mastered the proper technique in the job interview process to make you a success in your career regardless of what your job is? What if you could sit under the tutelage of someone who's been there; experienced it and succeeded at it? Think of how much time, energy and money you could save; how much pain you can avoid; how much money you could earn; and how much success you could achieve. All you need is the right teacher.

In competition, everyone experiences the thrill of victory and the agony of defeat. Everyone wins and losses in this competition called life. Everyone falls and rises in the process of learning. But why lose or fall when you can learn from someone else who has been through both—the failure and the success—and has mastered the technique of success?

In these chapters that follow, I will teach you the proper steps to a successful job interview. Before we jump in to those chapters, let's take a brief inventory of your competition.

Meet Your Competition:
US Government Employee and Contractor Workforce

By mid-year 2016, the Bureau of Labor Statistics reported there were 21.1 million total US government workers. Among this workforce, there are over 4 million federal, state and local government civilian employees, not counting civilians that work directly in the executive, legislative and judicial branches of the US government. On the other side of that government coin, you have over 10 million civilian government contractors who also work at the federal, state and local levels of our US government.

All of these government civilian employees and contractors are employed in over 500 US government departments and agencies both in the US and abroad in other countries. These government departments and agencies cover all areas of US governance. Areas such as transportation, telecommunications, health, education, agriculture, economy, finance, energy, commerce, postal service, drugs and alcohol, Peace Corps, labor, defense, veteran's affairs, homeland security, border patrol, science and international affairs. It's easy to see that a large portion of America's business sectors are made up of civilian government employees and government contractors. A complete listing of the US government departments and agencies and their contact information can be found at https://www.usa.gov/federal-agencies.

Military Veterans and Their Family Members as US Government Employees and Contractors

A large part of the US federal civilian employee and contractor workforce is former military members, in addition to spouses and children of active and retired military members. We all want to promote opportunities for our military and their family members after these brave men and women have served their country so well; and government employee and contractor job opportunities are avenues for the American public to give back to our military.

Former military members are oftentimes more willing and able to adapt to the restrictions placed upon civilians working in a government job or the changing working environment of the contractor world. After all, military members routinely change their tour of duty location every 2 to 5 years. They'll move to another state or another country, oftentimes bringing their family and household goods in tow with them; and begin working in a new military assignment for new bosses, new co-workers and new customers on a regular basis throughout their military career.

This "tour of duty" mentality was used by Reid Hoffman, the co-founder and executive chairman of LinkedIn, in his book, *The Alliance*, to explain a more realistic approach by employers and employees in accepting the fact that employment at one job, at one company, at one location isn't for life. According to Hoffman, the biggest lie that employers tell employees is that their employment relationship is for life like a family; and the biggest lie that employees tell employers is that their loyalty to the company is for life.

Working alongside our military as a defense contractor, I've witnessed on numerous occasions where military members served our country faithfully in a military uniform, and when it was time for them to leave the military, they simply changed clothing but not their job. In other words, they continued performing their same job in the government facility, but now they were performing these tasks as a government civilian employee or contractor instead of as a military member.

How is that possible? Because the same or similar job they were performing while serving in the military was also being performed by defense contractors or government civilian employees working alongside them. Upon their release from the military, these military veterans were immediately offered a civilian job—usually with an increase in pay—by a private company or a government agency in the same organization. It happens all the time.

I wish it would happen more often for our military veterans—**they deserve it!**

Naturally, the majority of people searching for jobs will not have the opportunity to land a job by simply transitioning from a military uniform to civilian attire while staying in the same workplace. Most of us have to go through the job search process and interviewing for a job.

Meet Your Competition: US Government Employee Workforce

US government employees, also referred to as federal employees or civil servants, are part of the US government called federal civil service that was established in 1871. They are civilians who work directly for and are paid by the US federal, state and local government. Besides the multitude of US government agencies and organizations where professionals work, the government employee workforce also includes the executive, legislative and judicial branches of government. Uniformed military services are not part of the civil service workforce.

4

The Office of Personnel Management (OPM)

All of the US federal, state and local government civilian employees are managed by the Office of Personnel Management (OPM). The OPM provides the following services to the government's civilian workforce:

- Recruits civilian candidates for government jobs by managing the government job announcements at the USAJOBS.gov website.

- Establishes and manages the standards used in the government recruitment and hiring process.

- Performs background investigations and maintains security clearances required for government jobs.

- Manages and controls the merit system used in promotions within the government civilian employee workforce.

- Manages and distributes benefits, such as health insurance and retirement pensions, offered to government employees and their families.

- Provides training and development programs to the government employee workforce.

The Application Process for US Government Employee Jobs

Welcome to Jurassic Park

As I guide you through the jungle of red tape wrapped around the axle of the US government employee job application process, I might as well introduce you to this section by saying, "*Welcome to Jurassic Park.*"

Ask any survivors of the US government application process and they'll probably respond with that deer in the headlight look and start to shake uncontrollably. Then they'll make a mad dash into the woods while screaming at the top of their lungs like the blonde-haired Lex Murphy, the young girl in the 1993 *Jurassic Park* film. That was her response when she first encountered the sofa-wide jaws and sharp fangs of the Tyrannosaurus Rex tearing open the jeep, like a can of tuna, where she and her little brother were hiding in.

As you enter the job-hunting jungle of the government's application process, crawling your way through the slush and muddied trail where prehistoric raptors work in paired hunting parties to devour job-hunting candidates' applications, resumes, documentations, time and effort; you'll soon feel more like the prey being hunted than the job hunter. Only the strong survive that process and live to talk about it.

What Doesn't Kill You Makes You Stronger

Don't get me wrong. My goal is not to discourage you from trying to seek a job with the US government. I'm preparing you for the journey you are about to embark on should you choose the career path of a US government employee. This journey requires an understanding of how the government's job application process works, and the patience and fortitude to persevere through this process. What doesn't kill you in the process will make you stronger.

It's not that the US government is intentionally trying to make their application process as difficult as climbing Mount Everest. They're just being . . . well, *the government.*

The government's modus operandi is layers of bureaucracy, and that is reflected in the way they process job applications. It's important to understand this because, compared to the application processes of private companies, the government's application process will make you feel like you just joined a Cirque du Soleil performance as you try to jump through all the hoops the government demands from job-seeking candidates submitting their applications online.

The jury is still out on whether or not the AcqDemo project, the new pay system currently being tested to replace the General Schedule (GS) pay system, will streamline the government hiring process enough for us to see a significant reduction in the time it takes to hire candidates for government positions. Until a quicker, more efficient job application process is in place, job seekers will have to endure the government's current job application process.

It requires a lot more stamina and patience to continue through the US government's online application process to the end. There are a lot more requirements, questionnaires and documentation you must provide to government agencies than you normally would to private companies for a job.

Most government agencies try to fill their open positions within 80 days or less from the date the job opening was posted. However, the waiting periods for multi-level reviews of multiple candidate applications and other required documents by government agencies can take several months compared to private companies that may only take weeks—all of that before you are considered for a job interview at the government agency.

The USAJOBS and Other Websites for US Government Jobs

All US government jobs are posted online in job announcements on a variety of websites. The official website for searching and applying for government jobs is at USAJOBS using the link https://usajobs.gov/. Normally, you have to create an account and profile on the website to apply for open positions the same way you have to for other online job boards.

USAJOBS.GOV

At the USAJOBS homepage, there are only two main search windows displayed: a **Keywords** search and a **Location** search window. The Keywords search window allows you to locate US government jobs by job title, skills, agency or other keywords. The Location search window allows you to locate US government jobs in the US or other countries, such as Italy, Germany, United Kingdom, Japan or South Korea. It's that simple. The search results will provide you a long list of open job opportunities to choose from. Just click on the job title in the list to learn more about the job and the application requirements.

Job announcements on these websites for US federal, state and local government positions typically include the following:

- The job title for the position.

- Number of vacancies for that particular position.

- Salary range for the position.

- Series & Grade stating the pay grade level for the position.

- Location of the job site.

- Open Period showing the date when the job announcement was first opened. The agency will accept applications during the open period.

- Closed Period showing the date when the job announcement is closed. The agency will no longer accept applications after the closed period.

- Announcement Number used as a tracking or reference number for the open job.

- The US government department, such as the Department of Defense.

- The agency within the government department, such as the Missile Defense Agency which is an agency within the Department of Defense.

- A summary of the government agency that is seeking candidates for the open job. This information explains what the mission of the agency is.

- Position or work schedule info, such as full-time.

- Who may apply, such as internal candidates only or open to all external candidates.

- The job description outlining the responsibilities of the position.

- Other pertinent information, such as whether or not travel or a security clearance is required for the position.

To search and apply for US federal, state and local government jobs, try some of the following websites:

- USAJOBS
  https://usajobs.gov/

- USAJOBS Resource Center
  https://help.usajobs.gov/index.php/Main_Page

- Feds Hire Vets
  http://www.fedshirevets.gov/

- America Jobs
  http://www.americajobs.com/

- USA.GOV
  http://www.usa.gov/Citizen/Topics/Government-Jobs.shtml

- US Postal Jobs
  http://bit.ly/2eaXDGK

- Army Civilian Service
  https://armycivilianservice.usajobs.gov/

- Army Civilian Service
  http://armycivilianservice.com/

- Air Force Civilian Jobs
  http://www.afciviliancareers.com/

- Air Force Civilian Jobs
  http://www.afpc.af.mil/

- Navy Civilian Jobs
  http://www.secnav.navy.mil/donhr/Pages/Default.aspx

- Navy Civilian Jobs
  https://don.usajobs.gov/

Meet Your Competition: US Government Contractor Workforce

US government contractors are civilians who work for and are paid by private companies, such as Boeing, Northrup Grumman, Lockheed Martin or a staffing agency that provides personnel, equipment and services to US government departments and agencies. Exceptions to this definition of contractors would be independent contractors who are self-employed individuals that do not rely on an outside company or staffing agency.

There are over 10 million civilian government contractors who work at the federal, state and local levels of our US government. It's common to see government contractors working alongside government employees and military personnel in the over 500 US government departments and agencies throughout the US and in overseas locations.

The government agency where the contractor works would be considered the primary company with the business need. However, the government contractor is employed by a private company (the secondary company) to meet the business need of the government agency. The government agency does not have direct control over the government contractor. The private company that pays the government contractor's salary and benefits has direct control over the contractor. Therefore, the IRS requires the contractor's employer—not the government agency—to withhold taxes from the contractor's earnings if the contractor is working under a W-2 tax form. Otherwise, contractors must track, record and withhold their own taxes for the IRS if they are using either a 1099 or Corp-to-Corp tax form.

The Application Process for US Government Contractor Jobs

Welcome to Disneyland Park

Compared to the *Jurassic Park* government employee job application process, the job application process for government contractors is like *Disneyland Park* (minus the expensive entrance fees).

The government contractor's entire hiring process is done through a private company or staffing agency. The people that interview and select the contractor for the government job are either from the private company that will pay the government contractor's salary or from other non-government corporations (such as contractors of another company that also work in the government agency). The contractor does not interact with the HR department or other government employees of the agency during the contractor's job application, salary negotiations, interview and selection processes. Therefore, the government contractor does not experience the months of delays and red tape associated with the government hiring process.

Contractors find government contractor jobs through the same online job websites as job-seekers in search of non-government private sector jobs, such as Monster.com, Indeed.com or CareerBuilder.com. Government jobs can also be found on the career links of a private company's website. You can apply for a specific government contractor job found on these sites or you can upload your resume to these job search websites so recruiters can contact you for government jobs that are currently available or will come available in the future.

Corporate and US government contracting jobs can be found at the following Internet job boards:

- Go to the website of the private company you are interested in working for and click on that company's Career link.

- Monster (for our United States readers)
  http://www.monster.com/

- Monster (for our international readers)
  http://www.monster.co.uk/geo/siteselection

- ClearedJobs
  http://clearedjobs.net/

- CareerBuilder
  http://www.careerbuilder.com/

- Indeed
  http://www.indeed.com/

- ClearanceJobs
  https://www.clearancejobs.com/

Meet Your Competition:
Corporate Employee and Contractor Workforce

Apart from the US federal employee and government contractor, we have the corporate employee and contractor workforce. You already know them as your first responders, healthcare providers, grocery store clerks, teachers, coaches, programmers, engineers, accountants, consultants, entrepreneurs, building contractors, mechanics, service providers, self-employed, home business, small and big businesses, non-profits, for-profits and a myriad of other non-public, non-government ventures that touch the fabric of everyday life in American society. They too can be your sons and daughters, your fathers and mothers, your sisters and brothers, your in-laws, your college graduates, and your military veterans. As a collective whole, we call them the private or commercial sector; and they are roughly 4 times the size of the US government labor force.

The US Bureau of Labor Statistics reported a 159 million total civilian labor force in mid-year 2016; and this figure is well on its way to a BLS projected growth of 164.4 million by 2020. If you are already in the private sector or are thinking of joining our ranks, then this book is for you too.

Meet Your Competition:
Corporate Employee Workforce

Corporate or private company employees are civilians who work for and are paid by non-government, non-staffing agency, private companies that own—or their shareholders own—that company's business. In other words, the paychecks and company benefits of these employees come directly from that business company, not from a US government agency or a staffing agency.

The company man.

These employees are what William H. Whyte, who first coined the term "groupthink" in *Fortune* magazine in 1952, introduced to the twentieth century public as *The Organization Man* in his 1956 bestseller book by the same name that sold over two million copies. These employees are often referred to as "permanent", "full-time", "company" employees, and "company man" or "company woman".

Their salaries are individual, negotiable contracts between the employee and the private business. Their salaries are based on the company's budgeted salary range for that position, documented qualifications (resume, certifications, degrees, skill level and years of experience), interview performance, and salary negotiation skills.

Meet Your Competition: Corporate Contractor Workforce

Corporate or private company contractors, on the other hand, are not considered as one of the full-time or company employees of a business (the primary company). They fall into either an independent contractor or dependent contractor role.

Independent Contractors

Independent contractors in the private sector are self-employed contractors providing products and/or services to individuals, groups, organizations and companies. They may receive payment from these clients or customers but they sign their own paychecks because they own their own business and they are their own boss. Consequently, independent contractors must track, record and withhold their own taxes for the IRS.

Dependent Contractors

Dependent contractors in the private sector are not self-employed. They work for a company or staffing agency that pays them their wages. If the dependent contractor is working under a W-2 tax form, the company or staffing agency will track, record and withhold taxes from their earnings for the IRS. If the dependent contractor is working under other tax forms, such as a 1099 or Corp-to-Corp tax form, they must track, record and withhold their own taxes for the IRS, just as independent contractors.

The remainder of our focus in this chapter will be on company employees and these dependent contractors that we'll simply call contractors. This group of non-company employees is oftentimes referred to as "contractor", "consultant", "freelancer" or "temporary" (temps) workers.

The name contractor is not a title given to only low or medium wage earners. Contractors include top managers and professionals, such as lawyers, doctors, Chief Executive Officers (CEOs) and Chief Financial Officers (CFOs). These contractors are called *supertemps* by Jody Greenstone Miller and Matt Miller in a Harvard Business Review article titled *The Rise of the Supertemp*.

Job-Hoppers and Jumpers

Many contractors are also humorously referred to as "jumpers". A jumper is a caricature taken from the 2008 film *Jumper* that was based on the 1992 science fiction novel written by Steven Gould that used the same title; telling the story of an individual who could jump from place to place through teleportation. In this context, a jumper is a term used to depict a contractor who moves from one job to another; in other words, a job-hopper.

In the *2016 Job Seeker Nation Study*, an annual report produced by Jobvite Inc., a software and recruiting corporation known for its surveys into social recruitment, between 34 and 35 percent of the 2,305 participants (aged 18+) in the 2016 survey reported they changed jobs after 1-5 years. Among this job-hopping group, those who are more likely to job-hop every 1-3 years are Millennials (ages 18-29) at 42 percent, 55 percent are millennial women and 31 percent are single people.

In their *2015 Recruiter Nation Survey*, Jobvite reported 30 percent of job seekers job-hopped every 1-3 years; 29 percent job-hopped every 4-6 years; 15 percent job-hopped every 7-10 years; and only 14 percent job-hopped every 10+ years.

It is clear that job-hopping is here to stay, and is popular across all industries in both public and private sectors.

Contractors are Free Agents

Contractors are what Daniel H. Pink, the former chief speechwriter for Vice President Al Gore, classified as part of the *Free Agent Nation* and expounded upon in his book by the same name in 2001. And like the free agents of your favorite professional football, basketball or baseball team, these free agent contractors roam more freely and more often from one company to the next with the opportunity of gaining more experience and making more money than their company employee counterparts.

Free agents

Although the IRS views most people in the film industry (actors, crew members and other people working on a film production) and professional athletes, coaches and staff of professional sports teams as employees instead of independent contractors; these people also move from one job to the next, one film to the next, and one team to the next just like contractors.

And yet, we call actors and professional athletes *free agents* who work through other agents in controlling multi-million dollar contracts they want for the film or team they play in. Why? Because in practice, most actors and professional athletes move from one job to the next just like any other contractor. Their normal career pattern is to move from one job to the next. One year they're gainfully employed on a film or team;

16

the next year they're unemployed without a film or team to speak of; and hopefully, the next time you see them, they're in another film or on another team again.

Wade Phillips, the National Football League (NFL) defensive coordinator for the 2016 Super Bowl 50 Champions, the Denver Broncos, was out of work in 2014. He was let go by the Houston Texans in 2013; he was a free agent looking for work. In 2015, he was hired as the defensive coordinator of what became one of the best defenses in NFL history during the 2015 regular season; and he was named the Assistant Coach of the Year in 2016.

Phillips started his NFL career with the Denver Broncos and made his rounds through five other teams—Buffalo Bills, Dallas Cowboys, New Orleans Saints, Atlanta Falcons and the Houston Texans—before he made his way back to Broncos Country in his coaching job. He's changed jobs more times than many contractors today. While being interviewed by reporters after the Broncos Super Bowl 50 win against the Carolina Panthers, Wade said, *"It was really special going from unemployed to winning the Super Bowl."*

Such is the life of free agent contractors that job-hop.

Contractors in the Corporate World

Contractors in the private sector may provide the same or similar services as a company's full-time employees, but they work for and are paid by a secondary company that has a business relationship with the parent or primary business company—the client.

If you've worked in the contractor workforce for any length of time, you know it is common practice for a single secondary company or multiple subcontractor companies to work in partnership with one primary company, referred to simply as the prime. These secondary companies can be either smaller or larger than the parent or prime company.

Besides your typical secondary company, such as Boeing, SAIC or Verizon, that can provide personnel, services and equipment to a prime company; secondary companies can also be staffing agencies whose sole purpose is to provide personnel for secondary or primary company clients.

Fortunately for contractors, there seems to be no end in sight of staffing agencies—also known as recruiting agencies or temp agencies—whose sole mission and purpose is to locate and provide qualified candidates as full-time company employees or contractors to businesses in both the public and private sectors.

Commercial contractors can be working either full-time (in terms of hours worked just like company employees) or part-time; and their salaries are negotiated in similar fashion as company employees. The main difference in salary negotiations of contractors and company employees is that contractors, who usually work directly for and are paid by a secondary company such as a staffing agency or subcontracting company, negotiate their hourly rate or salary with the secondary company instead of with the primary business company client as company employee hires would do.

There are both internal and external staffing offices. Internal recruitment offices use company employees, such as the human resource (HR) department of the company, to recruit employees from within the company, through promotions or position changes. Oftentimes, companies will use internal recruitment first to fill available slots, but if that is unsuccessful, companies will seek help from external recruitment agencies to find candidates for the job. Staffing agencies are external recruitment companies whose main purpose is to connect business needs with qualified personnel who can meet those needs.

Although you will encounter staffing agencies that will do their utmost to connect you to a client (private company or US government agency with the job opening), it's important to realize that whether you are dealing with an internal recruiter of a company or an external staffing agency, they both work for the employer (company client), not for you (the job-hunter).

This does not mean you cannot have a meaningful, professional, repeat relationship with a recruiter of a staffing agency who is helping you land a job. It just means the staffing agency's bread is being buttered by the employer, not you. Therefore, your relationship with a staffing agency recruiter is similar to the relationship a person who is looking to buy a home has with a real estate agent who is representing the seller of the home, not the buyer of the home.

The company client—not the staffing agency—is also the one who is ultimately providing your salary. If you get hired for a job through a staffing agency, the company paying your salary and benefits could be either the staffing agency or the private company client (or US government agency) the staffing agency connected you with. Whichever way you collect our paycheck, the money is originating from the employer with the job opening, not the staffing agency.

Meet Your Competition: Seasonal or Holiday Job Seekers

While some people are rushing to buy that turkey on sale or gifts at discount prices during the holidays, other people are rushing to those seasonal or holiday jobs. Whether it's Easter, Thanksgiving and the following Black Friday, Christmas or New Years; finding jobs during these holiday seasons are all about timing, like catching a wave on a surfboard.

Before we dive into the specifics of finding jobs during the holiday seasons, let's first take a broader view of when employers are hiring throughout the year.

Ride the Wave of Seasonal Hiring

Statistics show that company hiring practices occur in cycles or waves throughout the year. According to most statistics, the two biggest times in the year when companies in the majority of industries hire people the most are January and February and late September and October. These are the months after the Christmas and New Year holidays (for January and February) and after the summer break (for September and October) when the demand for workers exceeds the supply of workers.

January is the month when most companies receive their approved budgets for the new financial year. Additionally, everyone—including hiring managers and interviewers—has returned back to work after the holidays. This means companies have the money and resources in place to start interviewing and hiring new people again.

Hiring picks up in September and October because workers are returning from summer vacations. Companies know if they're going to hire people, they have to do it before their employees—particularly hiring managers and interviewers—begin their next round of vacations during the November and December holiday months.

Towards the end of each year, companies are also seeking tax write-offs to reduce taxes they owe on their profits that year. One of the ways companies do this is through increasing their costs for recruitment which is a tax write-off. It makes sense for companies to pay for more recruiters and new employees during the September and October months because their hiring managers and other interviewers will be at work during these recruiting months before they start taking time off from work again during the holiday season in November and December.

This doesn't mean you can't find jobs outside of these months. It just means these are the biggest hiring months overall across most industries in the US.

This is important to know especially when you want to increase your salary in your next job search. These months are a good time for job-hunters to ask for that higher salary because demand exceeds supply during these months. This information is also important if you've been out of the job market for a while and want to know when is a good time to jump back into the job market and catch the biggest wave of hiring activity to increase your chances of being hired. It's right at the beginning of January or at the beginning of September.

Start your job search at the beginning of the hiring cycle.

For those who work in industries that rely on warm summer conditions, such as construction, air conditioning, amusement parks and tourism; the best time to get hired first before other job-seeking candidates is at the beginning of the summer hiring cycles in these industries.

The US Bureau of Labor Statistics (BLS) Job Openings and Labor Turnover Survey shows spring and summer job openings on average each year start rising from a low in March to a peak in April; and then drop again in May. Then job openings rise again from May to a peak in July, at which time job openings decline again in August.

So if you want to get hired in the spring months, start looking for work at the beginning of March until hiring peaks in April. If you want to get hired in the summer months, start looking for work at the beginning of May until hiring peaks in July.

The months of June, July and August can oftentimes be the toughest time to get an interview for a job because hiring managers and other members on the interview team are taking their summer vacations. When one or two key people are missing from the interview team, companies usually wait till everyone is back at work before starting the interview process. You can find jobs during these summer months, but just be prepared for greater delays in the interviewing process because of these reasons.

Although November (Thanksgiving and Black Friday) and December (Christmas and New Year) may see an increase in holiday jobs in retail, overall hiring during these months are usually at their lowest levels of the year across major industries due to businesses slowing down for the holiday season and workers taking holiday and vacation days off from work.

Catch the Holiday Wave of Hiring

A great way to supplement your income or have extra spending money during the holidays is to catch the holiday wave of hiring between Thanksgiving and Christmas.

Contrary to the information about the slowdown in hiring across most industries during November and December, these winter months also see a hiring increase in certain industries such as retail stores between Thanksgiving and Christmas. Retailers in clothing, jewelry, sporting goods, electronics and holiday gifts increase their workforce during the higher volume sales months of November and December. Included in this list are restaurants, party suppliers, holiday decoration centrals, and winter attractions such as ski resorts. Other markets that seek out extra help during the winter holidays are post offices and other warehouse, fulfillment center, shipping and transportation companies, and online distributers because consumer spending has moved from brick-and-mortar toward click-and-order.

The National Retail Federation (NRF) provided the *2015 Holiday Trends and Expectations Survival Kit*, a report on holiday forecasts, consumer trends, historical retail sales data and employment data. This report shows holiday employment rose from a low 263.8 thousand workers when our US economy tanked in the 2008 recession to a high of over 700 thousand people working during the holidays in 2014 and 2015; and expected holiday hiring to reach 750 thousand people during the November and December months in 2016.

Many companies start preparing for this holiday rush by hiring more people for temporary work (part-time and full-time) as early as August or September for the final two months of the year. Most of these jobs are temporary because companies only need the extra personnel to handle the increase of customers during the holidays. Once the customer traffic and buying dies down, so do these positions.

The US Department of Commerce reported 2.9 million jobs were filled in the temporary help services industry in 2015. Although these jobs are only temporary, it gives many people an opportunity to gain experience and skills; network with people in the workforce; build their resume; and possibly open the door to a permanent position with the company. Don't forget the discounts you'll receive with many companies while working there.

Where to Look For Holiday Jobs

You don't have to search or drive far for holiday jobs because many of these retailers and other businesses are in your local neighborhood. Therefore, you don't necessarily have to search for these jobs at Internet job search websites. Just go to the retailer of your choice and ask about any job openings and apply for the job in person.

The following list is where you can apply for seasonal or holiday jobs for the November and December consumer rush. Don't wait until November to start applying for these jobs. Start inquiring about these holiday jobs in September and October.

- **Toys R Us**: They plan to hire around 40,000 seasonal workers in 2016.

- **Kohl's**: They plan to hire around 69,000 seasonal workers in 2016.

- **Target**: They plan to hire around 77,500 seasonal workers in 2016.

- **JCPenny**: They plan to hire around 49,000 seasonal workers in 2016.

- **Macy's**: They plan to hire around 83,000 seasonal workers in 2016.

- **Walmart**: If 2015 was any indication of how many people Walmart plans to hire in 2016 and beyond, you can expect Walmart to hire around 60,000 seasonal workers.

- **Party City**: They plan to hire around 35,000 seasonal workers in 2016.

- **Amazon**: If 2015 was any indication of how many people Amazon plans to hire in 2016 and beyond, you can expect Amazon to hire around 100,000 seasonal workers.

- **UPS**: They plan to hire around 95,000 seasonal workers in 2016; and even better news is that 37 percent of their seasonal hires in 2015 became regular UPS employees.

- **FedEx**: They plan to hire around 50,000 seasonal workers in 2016.

- **Santa Claus**: (I couldn't resist putting this in here.) According to an AARP article titled *12 Great Holiday Jobs* by Kerry Hannon, the contract pay range for Santas is from $10 to $200 an hour during the Christmas holiday season. Even Santa is making some jingle during the holiday season.

The following list is online job boards where you can find seasonal or holiday jobs:

- Snagajob
  http://www.snagajob.com/c/seasonal-jobs

- Backdoorjobs
  http://backdoorjobs.com

- CoolWorks
  http://www.coolworks.com

- Indeed
  http://www.indeed.com/q-Seasonal-jobs.html

- Go to the website of the company, such as Amazon.com, and apply on their career link.

Meet Your Competition:
Workforce Living and Working Overseas

Imagine spending your weekends or holidays taking in the panoramic view of the city of Paris from the top of the Eiffel Tower; stepping where battle-worn gladiators and 65,000 blood-thirsty Roman spectators had trodden in the ancient Coliseum in Rome; visiting the Alps in Switzerland, Austria, Italy or Germany to ski breathtaking slopes, picnic beside luminous lakes or tour enchanting villages and countryside; feeling the warm sand between your toes and the cool breeze through your hair (providing you have hair) on the spacious, lovely beaches of the French Riviera while time stands still as you relax at this European vacation spot; or feeling the excitement in the air while tourists gather to watch the royal guard and marching band dressed distinctively in tall black bearskin fur headgear, historic red coats and black pants nicely trimmed with red stripes marching proudly in step during the Changing of the Guard at Buckingham Palace.

Rather than spending an expensive and exhaustive family trip to see Disneyland's Sleeping Beauty Castle or ride the Matterhorn Bobsleds in America; living in Europe allows you to take your time on inexpensive day trips to walk through real castles, such as the luxurious Neuschwanstein Castle in Bavaria which Disney modeled their castle after; or take a breathtaking train ride to see the real Matterhorn mountain straddling the border between Switzerland and Italy.

Instead of dreading another long line of Black Friday bargain hunters and last minute Christmas shoppers pushing and shoving in city malls throughout the US; imagine friends and families laughing as they snuggle together seated at a table while feasting on bratwurst, gingerbread or other delicious treats and drinking cups of heartwarming Glühwein (warm red wine with spices, citrus fruits and sugar); or casually strolling through holiday lighting, decorations, holiday music, gifts, toys and the inviting smell of delicious food cooking at stalls and booths outside at a Christkindlesmarkt (Christmas market) under Germany's crisp, winter's night sky that sparkles with the twinkle of ol' Saint Nick's watchful eye. *Das ist wundervoll!* (That is wonderful!)

During Mardi Gras, you could rub shoulders among revelers adorned with beads in New Orleans; or you could celebrate Carnevale in Venice, Italy with partygoers, young and old, wearing colorful and elaborate costumes and masks of the 14th to 16th century era while strolling through the famous Piazza San Marco (Saint Mark's Square). You say you don't like crowds? Off in the distance, couples in lovers embrace are reclining in Venetian gondolas as they float their cares away across the calm, romantic waters of the Grand Canal.

Having lived and worked in Europe over 15 years, I've been able to see and do all of these things I just mentioned. It was easy and cheap because I lived and worked there; and so can you.

The advantages and disadvantages to living and working overseas are plentiful. Before we jump into some of those advantages and disadvantages, let's get a few definitions out of the way first.

Expatriates

Americans who relocate, temporarily or permanently, to foreign countries are called expatriates or expats for short. Expatriate comes from the two Latin words *ex* meaning "out of" and *patria* meaning "country" or "fatherland".

The term expatriate does not necessarily mean you are an "ex-patriot". A patriot is someone who loves and strongly supports or fights for their native country. An ex-patriot is simply someone who is the opposite of that definition; someone who no longer loves or supports their native country but instead has renounced their country.

"Expatriate" is not the same as "ex-patriot". Expatriates or expats still love and support their native country; they've just chosen to live and work temporarily or permanently in a foreign country. Whether or not a person still loves and supports their country is a personal patriotic choice; but the word expatriate is not the definition of that choice.

The US uses the term expatriate to classify non-federal employees living and working overseas, such as government contractors or employees of private companies living and working overseas. US government employees and Foreign Service employees are not considered expats.

The US Foreign Service is the part of the US Department of State that carries on US diplomatic functions in 265 overseas locations, called US diplomatic missions. You know many of these locations as US embassies and consulates where US diplomatic representation and services are performed by roughly 15,000 US professionals.

The difference between an expatriate and an immigrant is that immigrants always relocate to another country with the intent to take permanent residence in that foreign country. An expatriate's intention for relocating to another country is less concrete. Expats are either in that foreign nation only temporarily for work or education purposes; or expats could choose to remain there permanently but still retain their US citizenship.

The words emigrate and immigrate are two verbs describing different phases of the same process of becoming an immigrant. To emigrate means to leave a country to live in another foreign country permanently—it has to do with the exit part of the process of immigration. To immigrate means to enter a foreign country to live permanently after having left another country—it has to do with the entrance part of the process of immigration.

An immigrant and migrant is not the same thing either. Migrants are people who move from one place to another within the same country, such as an American living in California migrating to Colorado to live. Immigrants move between different countries.

The United Nations performs a variety of surveys on the world's population. In the UN report on immigrants, titled *International Migrants Stock Dataset in 2015*, 244 million people immigrated to another nation in 2015, an increase of 71 million people since 2000.

The US is not the only country that has expatriates or expats. Every country has expats—citizens of their own country living and working abroad in a foreign country.

The number of US expats living and working abroad is unclear because US censuses do not include Americans living abroad. Therefore, there is limited information as to the exact number of Americans living in foreign countries. However, delegates of the Association of Americans Resident Overseas (AARO) headquartered in Paris, an international non-partisan association with members in 46 countries, were told by State Department officials in 2015 they estimated roughly over 7 to 8 million Americans (excluding military) are living and working overseas in 160-plus countries. This is double the size of roughly 4 million Americans who were estimated living overseas in 1999.

Foreign Earned Income Exclusion for Expatriates

I've already mentioned one of the main advantages of living and working overseas—it's easier and cheaper to see and enjoy the sights of places like Europe or Asia while living there.

Another more profitable reason for Americans living and working overseas is the foreign earned income exclusion the IRS gives expats. This exclusion allows expats that are US citizens and file a US income tax return to exclude or reduce their taxable income.

How much income can be excluded?

It's an income exclusion that is adjusted annually for inflation. In 2014, expats could exclude $99,200 from their annual income. In 2015 and 2016, that exclusion amount rose to $100,800 and $101,300, respectively. That means if your salary from an overseas job was $90,300 in 2016, you could exclude all of your $90,300 when filing your income tax return. ***Boom shakalaka***!

If you made $150,000 in 2016, you could exclude the maximum amount of $101,300 which means you only have to pay US taxes on $48,700. This is one of the main reasons why 7 to 8 million Americans have chosen to live and work overseas.

In addition to exclusion from tax on income earned overseas, the foreign earned income exclusion also allows expats to exclude or deduct a certain percentage of foreign housing expenses, or meals and overseas lodging provided by employers. This reduces your taxable income even further.

As I mentioned earlier, US government employees and Foreign Service workers are not considered expatriates. Therefore, US federal employees and Foreign Service employees living and working overseas are not allowed to use the foreign earned income exclusion when filing their taxes. However, these government employees and Foreign Service workers may receive some nontaxable allowances for overseas expenses; and may be eligible for tax deductions on some expenses that are greater than their nontaxable allowance. For Foreign Service employees, some of their allowances or deductions include expenses for travel, entertainment, gifts, and costs for official functions. These expenses are similar to the expenses of someone working for a private corporation on a business trip. After all, Foreign Service workers are on a business trip in a foreign country on behalf of their employer, the US Department of State—one very long business trip.

If you are interested in working overseas in the Foreign Service, here are a couple of websites to learn more about what they do, what are the requirements and tests, and how to apply for a Foreign Service job.

- https://careers.state.gov/work/foreign-service

- http://bit.ly/2dF14ao

In order for non-government employees and contractors to qualify for the foreign earned income exclusion, US citizens working overseas have to pass one of these two tests:

- **Bona fide resident test**: The expat was a bona fide resident of a foreign country for a full US tax year. A "bona fide resident" means you are residing or living in a foreign country, but your domicile (permanent residence) is still in the US.

- **Physical presence test**: The expat was outside the US for 330 days in any 12-month period. This means you can be in the US (such as a short vacation away from the foreign country) for no more than 35 days out of any 12-month period (365 days). For example, if you are in the US for 36 days while living and working in the foreign country in a 12-month period, you are automatically disqualified for the earned income exclusion.

Paying Income Tax to a Foreign Country

It's not all gravy when it comes to exemptions to income taxes while living and working overseas. Everything I mentioned so far has to do with US income taxes. The foreign country you are living and working in may also require you to pay income taxes.

The US has many tax treaties with foreign countries. Some of these treaties allow you to pay reduced or no income taxes to the foreign country. Without these treaties or if you do not fall within the qualifications of the treaty, you most likely will have to pay income tax to that foreign country.

Take Germany and Italy for instance. Those countries require US citizens living and working in their country to pay income taxes on income earned in their country. However, Germany and Italy have tax treaties with the US that exempts US military personnel and US government employees (not American contractors) from being taxed by their country. In order for US government contractors living and working in Germany or Italy to be exempt from that country's income tax, US contractors must qualify as "technical experts".

TESA

The criteria for meeting the technical expert status are defined in the Technical Expert Status Accreditation (TESA) agreement between the US and the foreign country. A technical expert under TESA is a US government contractor (not a US government employee who is automatically exempt from paying income taxes to Germany and Italy) who performs complex tasks of a technical-military or technical-scientific nature in support of US military forces in that foreign country. Administrative or blue-collar work would not qualify for the TESA accreditation.

TESA requirements vary slightly between Germany and Italy. Generally, the TESA criteria requires the person to have a degree, such as a bachelor's degree, a certain number of years of experience in a technical field, and be in a job considered essential for the operation and support of US military forces in that foreign country. The resume (written by the contractor) and the job description (written by the employer) also helps to identify the contractor occupying that position as technically qualified for TESA accreditation. Having a US government security clearance is not a requirement for TESA accreditation; therefore, you do not need a US security clearance to qualify for the TESA tax exclusion.

There are some conditions that can disqualify you from the income tax exclusion by the foreign country even though you previously met the TESA requirements. For example, if your status changes to a permanent resident of the foreign country, you can be subject to income tax by that foreign country.

Factors that identify you as a permanent resident of that foreign nation include marrying someone who is a citizen of that foreign country; your children are enrolled in that country's school system instead of an International School Service (ISS) or a US sponsored school (such as schools on US military installations) in that foreign country; owning property in that foreign country; or having an American spouse who is working in that country's local economy. All of these factors disqualify you for TESA status. Under these conditions, you would have to pay income tax to that foreign country.

How attached you become over time to that foreign country's lifestyle, people and culture can impact your income tax status while living and working overseas. Crossing the line in ways that negatively impact your tax status with that foreign country is like having a half-filled grocery cart with not one but two bad wheels at Walmart. Do you continue with the two bad wheels knowing the more you load the cart, the harder it will be to push it? Or do you empty the cart and start all over again with a new cart?

Many US government contractors who crossed the line chose to keep pushing that cart and ended up either returning to the US with a new foreign wife (or foreign husband) to avoid paying income taxes to the foreign country; or remaining in that foreign country and paying that country's income tax. Other US government contractors decided to empty and change their cart in order to avoid paying that country's income tax while remaining in that foreign country.

I've held US government contractor positions while living and working in foreign countries outside of the US; and was able to take advantage of both the US income tax exclusions under the foreign earned income exclusion law and exclusions from income tax of foreign countries under the TESA agreement I just explained. In my eyes, the advantages outweighed the disadvantages in those overseas locations (as long as I had a grocery cart with four good wheels).

The following is a quick overview of other advantages and disadvantages of living and working overseas:

Pros to Living and Working Overseas

- The US government agency or private company that hired you will pay for your flight tickets and other travel costs to your overseas location.

- The US government agency or private company will pay for the packing and shipping of your household goods and vehicle to and from the foreign country.

- Opportunity to have relatives and friends come visit you overseas for an experience of a lifetime.

- Getting paid housing allowance and cost-of-living allowances (COLA)—extra money your employer provides you on top of your salary to pay for housing and the costs of living in the overseas area.

- Some companies will pay for one or two vacation trips back to the US per year while you are living and working overseas.

- If working as a US government employee or government contractor, the military installation's Housing Office will provide you housing assistance. This office has a listing of homes for rent on the economy; and will help you with communicating with landlords and establishing the rental contract. The Housing Office will also provide you free loaner furniture (beds, couches, lamps, tables, etc.) and appliances (washers, dryers, stoves, refrigerators, etc.) to complete your home furnishings; as well as free delivery and pick-up services of these loaner items.

- The US government agency or private company will oftentimes pay for storage of household goods or a vehicle in the US if you plan to leave them in the US while you live overseas. If employers do not pay for this storage, you can deduct the first year's storage fees from your income tax as moving expenses for a new job.

- You can store your vehicle in the US and buy a cheap used car on the local economy of that foreign nation. This way you save wear and tear on your car in the US; and will have it available for you when you return to live in the US again.

- Your US dollar may be worth more or less depending on the exchange rate of that foreign nation. If your US dollars are worth more, you can buy food, gifts, souvenirs and other commodities for less money on the local economy.

- If you own a home in the US, you can rent out your home through a property management company so you can have another source of income to pay off your mortgage while you are living overseas.

- If you are a US government employee or government contractor, you will be allowed to purchase gas coupons that allow you to purchase gas for your vehicle at a reduced price on the local economy.

- If you are a US government employee or government contractor, you will be allowed to purchase value-added tax (VAT) exemption forms that allow you to purchase commodities on the local economy without having to pay that country's VAT tax on those products.

Cons to Living and Working Overseas

- You must obtain and maintain a current passport, work permit and possibly a visa depending on the country.

- This move will require a change of address to route your mail to your new address in the foreign country.

- Having to take your children out of the US school system and enroll them in a school within the International School Service (ISS) or in a school on a US military installation overseas. (The ISS is also a great job opportunity for teachers who want to work overseas with other international teachers.)

- Possibly having to learn the language spoken in that foreign country; and the challenge or difficulty in communicating with people in that country.

- Overseas areas, such as Europe, Asia and the Middle East use 220v power. Your electronic devices must have 110v/220v capability or you can bring or buy voltage converters that can convert the 220v power from outlets to 110v for your 110v devices. You'll also need to buy several adapters to convert the US power cord plug to the type of plug that works with outlet shapes used in foreign countries.

- Your smartphone may or may not work in these overseas locations depending on whether or not your mobile phone has the proper capabilities. Mobile phones typically use one of two types of radio systems: Code Division Multiple Access (CDMA) or Global System for Mobiles (GSM). The CDMA radio signal does not work with the GSM signal. In the United States, Sprint, Verizon and U.S. Cellular use CDMA; AT&T and T-Mobile use GSM. Most of the mobile phones used overseas are using the GSM radio signal.

- Many foods you are accustomed to buying in US stores may not be available in the stores of foreign countries.

- Purchasing an international driver's license to allow you to drive in the foreign country; and finding an insurance company that insures your vehicle for driving on roads in foreign countries.

- Learning the road signs and rules of the road; driving on the left side of the road (in some countries such as the UK, Japan and Australia); taking that country's driver's exam; and converting kilometers (KM) per hour to miles per hour in order to drive safely within the proper speed limit on the roads.

- Voting must always be by mail-in ballot. If you don't have a problem with that, then this can be a pro instead of a con.

- You may need immunization shots based on the location of the foreign nation.

- Possibly the need to use a mail order pharmacy to receive your medications.

- The cost of shipping pets overseas. There may be other requirements before your pet is allowed to enter the foreign country, such as quarantine, an import permit, Blood Titer test, microchip or a pet passport.

- Greater vigilance may be required in some populated areas due to heightened awareness of terrorism.

The employer who hires you will assist you with many of the requirements listed in these pros and cons. For instance, your employer will oftentimes provide you an overseas mailing address beforehand so you can forward your mail to your new mailing address prior to departing the US. Employers typically provide their new employees with information on schools to enroll their children; housing information and housing assistance; vehicle registration and driving information; and other important information needed upon their arrival. Additionally, co-workers at their overseas job will offer assistance and information as well; and show them around the area to help them get settled in.

Resources for Finding Overseas Jobs and Living Overseas

If you'd like to try living and working temporarily in foreign countries, such as Germany, Italy, Greece, Belgium, Switzerland, Netherlands, Sweden, Spain, Turkey, UK, Australia, New Zealand, China, Japan, South Korea or South Africa; you can do so through a variety of ways.

Working as a US government employee, government contractor or employee of a corporation is just some of the ways of making that dream of living and working overseas a reality. You can also join an overseas volunteer program such as the Peace Corps; get on an internship or exchange program; attend an international career fair such as Global Careers Fair; or stay on the move internationally by trying yacht or cruise ship jobs.

You can find out about overseas jobs with private companies through online job boards in similar fashion to finding jobs in the US. In your profile on these job sites, you should also indicate which overseas countries you are willing to work in.

Following are some of the online job boards where you can find overseas jobs in the private sector:

- LinkedIn.com
  https://www.linkedin.com

- One Day One Job
  http://www.onedayonejob.com

- OverseasJobs.com
  http://www.overseasjobs.com

- InternationalJobs.com
  http://www.internationaljobs.com

- GoAbroad.com
  http://jobs.goabroad.com

- TransitionsAbroad.com
  http://www.transitionsabroad.com

- Peace Corps
  https://www.peacecorps.gov

- Global Careers Fair
  https://www.globalcareersfair.com

- Seek
  https://www.seek.com.au

- Expat Network
  https://www.expatnetwork.com

- Theguardianjobs
  https://jobs.theguardian.com

- Yacht Jobs
  http://www.yacrew.com

- All Cruise Jobs
  http://www.allcruisejobs.com

- Oil Jobs Overseas
  http://www.airswift/as/oil-jobs-overseas

- TeachAway
  https://www.teachaway.com/teaching-jobs-abroad

There are also many helpful online resources providing support groups and information on how to live and work overseas.

Following are some online resources about living and working overseas:

- U.S. Passports and International Travel
  https://travel.state.gov/content/passports/en/abroad.html

- TransitionsAbroad.com
  http://www.transitionsabroad.com

- GoAbroad.com
  http://www.goabroad.com

- Go Overseas
  https://www.gooverseas.com

- British Universities North America Club (BUNAC)
  http://www.bunac.org

- Easy Expat
  http://www.easyexpat.com

- Expats Abroad
  http://www.expats-abroad.com

- Expat Network
  https://www.expatnetwork.com

- ExpatWoman
  http://www.expatwoman.com

- American Citizens Abroad
  https://www.americanabroad.org

- Escape Artist
  http://www.escapeartist.com

- My World Abroad
  http://myworldabroad.com

- Alliance Abroad Group
  http://allianceabroad.com

- Moving Worlds
  https://movingworlds.org

- InterNations
  https://www.internations.org

The Job Recruiters

For those of us job-hunters in search of available job openings, some ways to get our foot in the door are through company career websites, job fairs, professional networking and external staffing agencies. Sometimes staffing personnel come looking for us to work in an open position.

There are both internal and external staffing offices. Internal recruitment offices use company employees, such as the human resource (HR) department of the company, to recruit employees from within the company, through promotions or position changes. Oftentimes, companies will use internal recruitment first to fill available slots, but if that is unsuccessful, companies will seek help from external recruitment agencies to find candidates for the job. Staffing agencies are external recruitment companies whose main purpose is to connect business needs with qualified personnel who can meet those needs.

Although you will encounter staffing agencies that will do their utmost to connect you to a client (private company or US government agency with the job opening), it's important to realize that whether you are dealing with an internal recruiter of a company or an external staffing agency, they both work for the employer (company client), not for you (the job-hunter).

This does not mean you cannot have a meaningful, professional, repeat relationship with a recruiter of a staffing agency who is helping you land a job. It just means the staffing agency's bread is being buttered by the employer, not you. Therefore, your relationship with a staffing agency recruiter is similar to the relationship a person who is looking to buy a home has with a real estate agent who is representing the seller of the home, not the buyer of the home.

The company client—not the staffing agency—is also the one who is ultimately providing your salary. If you get hired for a job through a staffing agency, the company paying your salary and benefits could be either the staffing agency or the private company client (or US government agency) the staffing agency connected you with. Whichever way you collect our paycheck, the money is originating from the employer with the job opening, not the staffing agency.

When a staffing agency initially contacts you, the person communicating with you is usually a recruiter. Recruiters are the first line staffing personnel who make the initial contact with potential job-hunting candidates. Recruiters have various job titles, such as Executive Search Consultant, Professional Recruiter, Staffing Consultant, Recruiter, Sourcing Agent, Technical Recruiter, Senior Talent Delivery Strategist, Tech Rep or Recruiting Partner.

There are a plethora of recruiters in today's job market. That surplus of recruiters, both locally and out-of-state, allows you to be selective on which recruiters you want to work with, especially once you learn how to make recruiters seek you out for job openings and not the other way around. Although staffing agency recruiters are working for the employer, stick with recruiters that make you feel as though they are working for you and avoid the rest.

Retained and Contingency Recruiters

Recruiters operate in one of two categories with company clients: retained or contingency.

Retained Recruiters

Recruiters working on a retained basis with a company client means the company is giving that recruiter exclusive rights to fill their job openings. The company client will not accept resumes from their internal (HR) recruiters, other staffing agencies, candidate applications submitted directly to the employer's career website, or any other channels the employer can get resumes. The company client may even have the retained recruiter on an annual contract basis.

Retained recruiters may seem more personable and patient than contingency recruiters because they don't have to compete with other staffing agencies for the employer's available positions. They will take more time to ensure the candidate is the best fit for the employer.

When employers use retained recruiters, it typically means the recruiter's staffing agency has developed a long-standing, trusted relationship with the company. It's an expensive relationship though because employers pay up to 50 percent of a candidate's projected first annual salary to retained recruiters. However, the employer is confident that this staffing agency can find them the quality professionals they're looking for. Because of this expense, employers typically use retained recruiters for more experienced or senior positions instead of junior positions to get a greater return on their investment.

When the employer needs to fill a position, the retained recruiter may present between 3 to 10 candidate resumes, along with each candidate's salary expectation, to the employer to choose from to interview.

When the retained recruiter asks for your permission to submit your resume to an employer, your resume may actually be one of several resumes the recruiter is submitting to the employer for the same job opening. This is important to know because, although the recruiter and the employer may have agreed to your desired salary, if your skill sets and qualifications are similar to the other candidates the employer is interviewing for the same job, the employer may select the candidate with the lower salary. This way, the employer saves money by hiring the candidate with the lower salary resulting in a lower commission for the retained recruiter.

It's good to be able to ask for more, but sometimes less is more, especially when you are competing with other candidates with similar skill sets and qualifications as you for the same position.

Contingency Recruiters

When a recruiter works on a contingency basis with a company, this means the recruiter is competing with other staffing agencies; the employer's internal (HR) department; applications submitted directly to the employer's career website by job-hunting candidates; and from other channels the employer is willing to accept resumes.

Contingency recruiters operate on a "no win, no fee" or "no cure, no pay" basis with employers. This means contingency recruiters only get paid a commission if their candidate is hired by the employer. Their commission is typically between 10–25 percent of the candidate's projected first annual salary.

As with retained recruiters, when the contingency recruiter asks for your permission to submit your resume to an employer, your resume is actually one of several resumes the recruiter may be submitting to the employer for the same job opening.

You can tell when recruiters are working under a contingency basis with an employer when you receive multiple calls or emails from several recruiters of different staffing agencies about the same job opening. It's basically first come, first served—the recruiter who can get the best resumes in the hands of the employer first will get those resumes looked at first. That's why there is such a rush of recruiters trying to reach out to you about the same job. Their rush job makes contingency recruiters appear less personable and less patient than retained recruiters. They simply do not have the luxury of time and exclusivity that retained recruiters have to find the right candidate for available job opportunities.

Recruiter Alliances

The life of a contingency recruiter can be a dog-eat-dog world with so many recruiters competing for the same job-seeking candidates and available job openings. So instead of going it alone, some recruiting agencies have learned over time that there is safety—and commissions— in numbers. Like wolf packs that instinctively hunt their prey in groups, these headhunters hunt in packs to increase their chances of success in getting a commission. These recruiters have learned to headhunt together through recruiter networks or alliances; and when their teamwork results in a commission, they will share the profits 50–50.

These contingency recruiters will form into networks or alliances in order to share job listings and potential job-hunting candidates. This allows them to spread a wider net in finding open jobs and candidates to fill those jobs. Like the rest of the animal kingdom, these recruiters have learned to adapt to their working environment in a way that enables them to control more of that competitive recruitment environment.

The Recruiter's Commission

Employers pay a commission fee or flat rate to staffing agencies for finding professionals to fill available positions. Although we speak of the commission as being a recruiter's commission, the recruiter actually receives only a percentage of the commission that the employer pays to the staffing agency.

For retained recruiters, the commission paid to staffing agencies by employers is typically between 40–50 percent of the candidate's first annual salary. For example, if your negotiated annual salary is $80K a year, the employer will pay the staffing agency $40K at a 50 percent commission rate. If your negotiated annual salary is $120K a year, the employer will pay the staffing agency $60K at a 50 percent commission rate.

For contingency recruiters, the commission paid to staffing agencies by employers is typically between 10–25 percent of the candidate's first annual salary. For example, if your negotiated annual salary is $80K a year, the employer will pay the staffing agency $20K at a 25 percent commission rate. If your negotiated annual salary is $120K a year, the employer will pay the staffing agency $30K at a 25 percent commission rate.

Staffing agencies understand that if you don't get hired, they don't get paid. It is in the staffing agency's best interest to provide you the best service possible in helping you land that job you're looking for; and the higher your salary is, the greater their commission.

Some recruiter commissions are structured on the number of candidates they can place in job openings, and not necessarily on the

44

quality of candidates placed in those positions. This leads some recruiters to behave more like headhunters than professional recruiters in their pursuit of greater commission compensation. For this reason, you need to be smart about the recruiter you are dealing with.

Since staffing agencies are being paid by employers, there is no reason for you to pay staffing agencies for their service in helping you find a job. So avoid those agencies that require you to pay them a fee for assisting you in your job search. Employers may also pay staffing agencies based on the contractor's hourly billings for the duration of the contract. Some staffing agencies are paid a fee by companies regardless if the candidate is hired or not, such as staffing agencies with exclusive rights with a corporation to find candidates for that company.

CHAPTER TWO

Interview Preparation and Tips

I will prepare and some day my chance will come.
Abraham Lincoln

As with many things in life, preparation is one of the keys to success. Preparation is the action behind the belief that one day, some day your chance will come to put that preparation to use. Without it, all plans, great and small, can fail. No matter how educated, gifted, talented, smart, experienced or resourceful you are—***you need preparation***. This is also true when it comes to your next job interview; whether it is a phone interview or in-person interview.

You've researched the career paths—US government agencies and private companies—and have made your selection of the job sector you will pursue. You've uploaded your resume on Internet job search websites and talked with recruiters. You've negotiated your salary with a recruiter and they submitted your resume to the employer. You beat out most of the competition from other staffing agencies, resumes and candidates; and the employer would like to interview you.

Now you have an appointment for a job interview in the next couple of days—***Congratulations***!

Everything you've done up to this point was for that job interview, but the competition doesn't end here. You are still in competition with other candidates during the interview process; and as with many job openings, only one person is going to get the job. So now is not the time to sit back, rest on one's laurels and wait for the day of your interview to arrive.

There's work to be done—it's called **pre-interview preparation**.

Carli Lloyd is the professional midfielder soccer player and co-captain of the US women's national soccer team; scoring the famous three goal hat trick within 16 minutes in that final match against Japan that won the 2015 FIFA Women's World Cup championship among 23 other international teams. She is also a two-time Olympic gold medalist and the 2015 FIFA Player of the Year. When it comes to preparation, Lloyd said, *"The harder you work and the more prepared you are for something, you're going to be able to persevere through anything."*

The same is true when it comes to preparing for your job interview.

Start With an Attitude of Gratitude

If you had a staffing agency help you get that job interview, your first order of business should be to thank your staffing agency recruiter or account manager for setting up your interview. In the excitement of being notified that the hiring manager wants to interview you, don't forget to take the time to thank the staffing agent that set up that all-important job interview for you. Show the staffing agent you are a classy professional by expressing your appreciation for their efforts thus far. This can be done by a simple thank you to the staffing agent over the phone following them giving you the good news about an interview or you can send a thank you email or text to the agent if you've been communicating online.

First Impressions Are Lasting Impressions

The job interview is all about making a good impression on the hiring manager and your interviewers. It starts with your first impression upon your arrival at the interview—by phone or in-person—and continues throughout your interview to your last impression at the end of your job interview.

The old saying *first impressions are lasting impressions* is perhaps never more repetitively impactful in your adult life than with job interviews. The first impression you display at your job interview could mean the difference between you owning a home or losing one; paying off your debt or watching the bills pile up; having it or losing it; only dreaming it or actually living it; starting over or going under— **impactful**. Only you know just how impactful your next job interview is to you, to your loved ones and your place and status in life.

The job interview as a whole is the first and perhaps only opportunity you have to make a good enough impression on those interviewing you to influence them to either hire you for the job or invite you back for a second interview.

I'm going to help you in your preparation to make as good of an impression as you can. That's what this chapter is about.

Give Yourself Time to Prepare for the Job Interview

With preparation comes familiarity and a renewed level of normalcy in the thing prepared that produces better results, greater confidence and comfortability when you move from preparation to application. Therefore, you want to be as prepared as you possibly can before you go into the job interview so that what you are experiencing during the interview feels as familiar and normal as possible to you. This will make you feel more confident and comfortable throughout the interview process. However, preparation takes time.

In this chapter, we're going to take the time to ensure you have all the information you need to know before an upcoming job interview; what you should research ahead of time; how to make a good impression with your hiring manager and other interviewers on the phone or in the interview room; how you should dress for success; and what you should be prepared to say. This information will help you cover all the important key areas that will give you the greatest chances for success in your next job interview.

In chapter 3, I'll go over all the details you need to know about the dynamics of job interviews when you are actually on the phone or in the room with the interviewers; how to conduct yourself and respond in the interview to make the best impression; what things you should focus on and talk about; and what the interviewers are looking for in your answers.

I've been down this road many times and have learned what it takes to be prepared for job interviews. I'm completely confident and comfortable every time I speak in a phone interview or go into a job interview because I've learned the secrets to preparing well for interviews. Now I'm going to show you how to do the same thing in these next two chapters. So rest easy; you're in good hands. (Sorry if that sounded like an Allstate commercial.)

After the staffing agency recruiter or account manager informs you that the hiring manager wants to interview you, they will ask you when you can come in for an interview (if it is an in-person interview), or when can you be interviewed over the phone. You should tell them you can interview in 2–3 days. This will allow you sufficient time for preparation, researching and planning for this interview. You should also provide a specific timeframe that fits into your work schedule (if you are employed) or personal schedule. If time is not a factor for you, you can tell the staffing agency that you will accept whatever time fits in best for the interviewer's schedule.

Do not ask for a week or more before you are ready to interview. Waiting this long will make the interviewers think you are either not interested in the job or are interviewing for other jobs before them; both of which will reflect poorly on you.

Sometimes the interviewers are under a tight interview schedule because of the number of candidates they are interviewing or due to their work priorities. In this case, the interviewers will provide you dates and times for your interview, and you simply have to pick one of those appointments.

Once you've given the staffing agency recruiter or account manager your desired interview date and time, the staffing agency will forward your requested interview appointment to the employer. If there are any conflicts in schedules, the staffing agency will let you know.

If all parties can make it to your interview appointment, the staffing agency will send you a confirmation email. This email usually includes the names of some or all of your interviewers; the address of the interview location (if it is an in-person interview) or the phone number to call (if it is a phone interview); and the scheduled date and time all parties have agreed to be present for your interview.

The following list is the key areas you should focus on when preparing for your upcoming interview:

- Appearance and attire

- The company client

- The interviewers

- The job description

- Your resume for the interview

- Certification's and experience's place in interviews

- Education's place among successful people

- Arrival at your interview

- Introductions in your interview

- Interview questions and answers

- Questions to ask the interviewers and closure

- Role playing interviews

Appearance and Attire for Job Interviews

What better way to start off our discussion about first impressions than with appearance and attire; but first a reality check.

Many employers prefer to have their first interview with you over the phone instead of in person. If this is the case, the staffing agent will let you know, and you will not have to concern yourself with this section on appearance and attire for that interview. We'll get into more specifics of the phone interview in chapter 3.

However, if the interviewers like how you answered their questions over the phone, they're going to ask you to come in for a second in-person interview. If the latter is true and the hiring manager wants you to come in for an in-person interview; then that's when this section on appearance and attire will matter to you most.

How Your Appearance and Attire Makes an Impression

Whether you are asked to come in for an in-person interview once, twice or three times, you should always dress as professional in your second and third interviews as you would for the first. If you are dressed appropriately, this will start your interview off on the right foot. What you are wearing is the first thing your interviewers will notice when you arrive for the interview. Your appearance will form their first of many first impressions of you within seconds of your first meeting.

The staffing agency recruiter or account manager who submitted your resume may also be meeting you for the first time at the employer's facility. If you are dressed unprofessionally, the staffing agency may be hesitant about submitting your resume for other positions in the future if you do not pass this interview. After all, the way you are dressed not only affects the employer's impression of you, your attire is a reflection on the staffing agency's ability to find quality professionals who can dress appropriately for job interviews.

If you've been to a lot of job interviews as I have, it's not long before you notice that every time you show up for the interview looking your best in your professional-looking business suit or outfit, the interviewers are always wearing the typical casual dress that people normally wear to work. If you work in the IT industry as I do, you know the look: khaki pants; worn buttonless short sleeve shirt or casual button-down long sleeve shirt with the tails hanging out; and shoes that look a bit worse for the wear.

If you've felt a bit overdressed sitting there in that room in your suit while they all get to wear casuals; just remember one thing about that interview: it *is* all about you, not the interviewers. They've all been through what you're going through in the interview process and they got the job. They were working that morning long before you arrived for your scheduled interview; and they have to keep working long after you leave. In other words, they earned the right to wear those casuals. What they're doing now, sitting across from you in their casuals, is taking time out of their busy day to focus solely on you. You're the one looking for the job; it's all about you, so enjoy the attention they're giving you despite their busy work schedule.

Your interviewers will appreciate the fact that you took your interview seriously enough to dress appropriately for the occasion, just like they had to when they were interviewed for their jobs in that company. Your appropriate response in dressing well for this job opportunity is another good first impression, even though your interviewers appear to be underdressed for the occasion. After you are hired, you'll be back to wearing the same casuals as the rest of your interviewers.

How to Dress for Visits to Recruiter Offices

When the staffing agency is in your local area, the recruiter may ask you to come in to their office first before they arrange an interview between you and the company client. Typically, you wouldn't wear a suit and tie for these meet-and-greet recruiter interviews as you would for a job interview with the company client. However, this visit at the recruiter's office is still an interview—a pre-screening interview. As with the phone interview that I'll go over in detail in chapter 3, this requested visit to the recruiter's office is an *elimination process*, not a hiring process. Therefore, dress smartly if you plan to visit a job recruiter's office at their request.

The recruiter is asking you to come to their office because they want to see your personal appearance and how you present and conduct yourself. From the time you enter the staffing agency's door and shake the recruiter's hand until you say your goodbyes in departing; the recruiter will be evaluating your appearance and their own comfort level in introducing you to potential employers.

Based on how you look and act in this introductory meeting, the recruiter will make their final decision on whether they should submit your resume to the employer or not. Therefore, dress appropriately in a business casual outfit to these meetings with recruiters. You can use some of the guidelines I provide in this section to pick out certain colors and materials in your outfit that are just as appropriate for the recruiter meeting as they are for your actual in-person job interview.

If I decide to visit the recruiter at their office, I typically ask the recruiter if they'd like me to come in dressed in business casual or the suit I'll wear to the interview. This way, I'll know for certain how I should dress for this visit.

Dress for Success When Applying for Seasonal Jobs

Even though it may be only a seasonal or holiday job at Walmart, JCPenny, Target or another retailer; you should always dress appropriately when inquiring about an available seasonal position. Rules about first impressions apply when people at that retail store, especially the hiring manager, meet you for the first time. It doesn't matter if you're applying for a job at Home Depot and everyone there wears jeans. You're not one of their employees dressed for work. You're a person on the outside looking for a job on the inside. Hiring managers, including Home Depot hiring managers, expect you to dress neatly when you ask for a job application to work at their store.

When inquiring about job openings at Walmart, JCPenny, UPS or other businesses, a business suit for men or a business outfit for women is not required. However, you should be dressed neatly in business-casual attire, such as conservative neat slacks, a collared shirt (a tie is appropriate for clothing stores and other retailers where workers wear ties) and polished shoes for men; and conservative neat slacks or dress, blouse and shoes for women.

In this chapter, I'll go over in great detail the appearance and attire that is acceptable for both men and women seeking jobs in corporate and government job sectors. The advice I give in this chapter is about the industry standard for proper business attire that men and women should wear for those types of job interviews.

Prepare Your Attire Ahead of Time for the Job Interview

Once you have an appointment for an interview, one of the first things you should do is go over your business attire you plan to wear to the job interview. This is important because you may discover your business suit, outfit, skirt, shirt, blouse or shoes need cleaning, mending or replacing.

The cleaners can press and clean your clothes faster than their normal service but you'll have to pay a little extra for that. However, this still may take a day or two, hopefully in time before your interview.

Mending your clothes or shopping for something new also takes time. You do not want to be scrambling to accomplish these things the day of your interview when you're trying everything on. If you need to buy a business suit or business outfit, ask the salesperson at the clothing store for advice in picking out a conservative business suit or business outfit for a job interview. They'll be able to point you in the right direction— part of their job is to help make you look good for the right occasion.

Do yourself a favor and have a clean and pressed outfit set aside and ready for any job interview. Cover it in a plastic garment bag and hang it in your closet to keep it protected and free of lint or dust. You can purchase garment bags for as low as $6–$12 online or at your local shopping center.

Although I have several suits, I always have one suit with a clean white shirt that I only use for job interviews, covered in a garment bag hanging in my closet. The day before my interview, I pull my suit out of the garment bag; pick out a tie, belt, socks and shoes; and try everything on once as a final check to make sure all of my clothing is ready to wear the following day of my interview.

Conservative is king.

When it comes to your selection and fashion of outfits, conservative is king for job interviews. You are attending a business function, not a night out on the town or a party. Therefore, your choice of colors, material, fashion and fit in your attire should reflect this business event.

There may also be organizations in your local area that provide assistance to job-seekers with their job interview attire. For example, in my city of Denver in Colorado, there is the *Dress For Success Denver* organization that helps provide women with a network of support, professional attire and development tools to give them the greatest chance to succeed and thrive in the workplace.

I've provided you a list of conservative dress for both men and women who are preparing for their next job interviews. These colors, materials, fashion and fit are tried and true conservative choices used in every industry for job interviews. You can't go wrong with these guidelines.

Recommendations for Men's Appearance and Attire for an Upcoming Job Interview:

- **Suit:** Well-fitting, clean and pressed two-piece single-buttoned business suit with matching jacket and pants made of natural fibers such as wool; in conservative colors, such as dark navy blue or charcoal (dark gray). Do not mix colors or materials in the jacket and pants. No missing buttons, lint or smell of smoke.

- **Shirt:** Clean, pressed (or ironed yourself) long-sleeved button-down shirt in white or light blue solid color or conservative stripes. No stains around the collar or missing buttons. [For recruiter meetings: other conservative colors are acceptable.]

- **Tie:** Conservatively designed silk tie that coordinates with your suit color. Avoid bow ties, flashy ties meant for parties or night clubs, and fashion extremes such as character ties.

- **Shoes:** Cleaned and polished conservative shoes in black, dark brown or cordovan (burgundy) matching the color of your belt. Shoes can be lace-up or slip-on business shoes.

- **Belt:** Conservative belt in black, dark brown or cordovan (burgundy) matching the color of your shoes.

- **Socks:** Conservative dark single-colored socks that coordinates with, and is equal to or darker than, your pants color. The socks color should not be lighter in color than your pants. Avoid multi-colored socks with different patterns.

- **Hair and Facial:** Hair should be clean, well-kept and cut if needed. Avoid extreme or unnatural-looking hair colors during the interview. Facial hair, such as beards or mustaches, should be neatly trimmed or cleanly shaven (no stubble look). This doesn't mean you can't ever grow the stubble look or a full beard; you should wait until after you are hired to do that (contractors and employees do this all the time). Clip visible nose hairs. You can purchase an electric nose clipper at your local shopping center. No hats.

- **Mouth:** Brush your teeth and don't eat after you have brushed; otherwise, brush your teeth again. Have fresh breath (breath mints or sprays can help in this area). Don't smoke right before your interview. No gum, candy or other objects in your mouth during the interview.

- **Hands:** Clean hands; fingernails cleaned and trimmed to short length. No gloves.

- **Tattoos:** Conceal visible tattoos if possible.

- **Fragrance:** Little to no fragrance, such as cologne, after shave lotion or hair scents. Wear deodorant. Avoid smoking while in your suit to prevent the smell of smoke when in the interview room.

- **Watch or jewelry:** Conservative, nice watch (if you choose to wear one). A finger ring is acceptable, such as wedding, engagement or school rings. Other than wedding and engagement rings, the ring should be conservative, not flashy. Avoid wearing stackable rings, midi rings or multiple rings on several fingers. Avoid necklaces, bracelets and leather wraps. Avoid jewelry with political, religious or designs or insignia representing a movement or lobby. No visible body piercings.

- **Accessories:** Clean and conservative notebook, portfolio or slim briefcase (for holding unfolded resumes, notepad and writing pen). The portfolio or briefcase should coordinate with the color of your shoes. No pictures promoting your favorite sports team, movie or other images on the notebook or carrying device. No backpacks or other book bags. The interviewers normally have their own copy of your resume they received from the recruiter; therefore, a simple small notebook or portfolio should do if you need to bring these things. No need to bring documents showing your previous work unless you are told to do so before the interview.

Recommendations for Women's Appearance and Attire for an Upcoming Job Interview:

- **Suit, Dress or Skirt:** Well-fitting, clean and pressed pant suit, skirted suit or, as a last choice, a dress and blouse under a blazer or jacket. Pant suit, skirted suit or dress should be made of natural fibers such as wool or wool blend; in conservative colors, such as dark navy blue or charcoal (dark gray). Other less used but acceptable colors is neutral colors, such as beige, brown or possibly dark red or burgundy. Jacket can be 1 or 2-button. Do not mix colors or materials in the jacket/blazer and pants. If using a jacket over a dress, ensure colors match well with each other. No missing buttons, lint or smell of smoke. Dress or skirt should be of moderate length, not above the knee.

- **Blouse:** Clean, pressed (or ironed yourself) long sleeve blouse made of cotton or silk in white or another light color such as pastel. [For recruiter meetings: other conservative colors are acceptable.] Avoid low cut or sheer blouses. No stains around the collar or missing buttons. No camisole tops.

- **Hosiery:** Clean in neutral color such as tan or sheer black. Avoid white nylons. No runs or holes.

- **Shoes:** Cleaned and polished, conservative, moderate height heels or pumps (1–1 ½ inch) or flats in black, dark brown or cordovan (burgundy) matching the color of your belt.

- **Belt:** If used, should be conservative in black, dark brown or cordovan (burgundy) matching the color of your shoes.

- **Hair and Facial:** Hair should be clean, conservative and worn in a comfortable fashion, yet a polished, stylish look that's free of frizz and flyaways. Wrapped sleek-looking ponytail or bun, top not or French twist are acceptable. Avoid hair styles that cover your face or eyes during the interview. Avoid extreme or unnatural-looking hair colors during the interview. Makeup should accentuate your facial features and make you feel confident and comfortable without overdoing it or going to extremes, such as in a runway fashion show. Avoid using eyeshadow, smoky eye, double wing, cut crease or cat's eye makeup to an interview (save that look for your night out on the town). Clip visible nose hairs. You can purchase an electric nose clipper at your local shopping center. No hats.

- **Mouth:** Brush your teeth and don't eat after you have brushed; otherwise, brush your teeth again. Have fresh breath (breath mints or sprays can help in this area). Don't smoke right before your interview. No gum, candy or other objects in your mouth during the interview.

- **Hands:** Clean hands with fingernails cleaned, unchipped and well-manicured. Nail polish, if used, should be a conservative neutral shade, such as sheer, taupe, beige, mild pink or clear nail polish. Avoid nail art, sparkles, neons and stripes nail polish for the interview. No gloves.

- **Tattoos:** Conceal visible tattoos if possible.

- **Fragrance:** Little to no fragrance, such as perfume, lotions or moisturizers, creams, hair spray or scents. Wear deodorant. Avoid smoking while in your outfit to prevent the smell of smoke when in the interview room.

- **Watch or jewelry:** Conservative, nice watch (if you choose to wear one). Small, simple, conservative earrings or studs in gold, silver, pearl or diamond are acceptable. Avoid big hoops, dangling or whimsical motif earrings. A finger ring is acceptable, such as wedding, engagement or school rings. Other than wedding and engagement rings, the ring should be conservative, not flashy. Avoid wearing stackable rings, midi rings or multiple rings on several fingers. A conservative, thin necklace in gold, silver, pearl, or small pendant are acceptable. Avoid layered or large necklaces and large pendants. Avoid bracelets, bangles and leather wraps. Avoid jewelry with political, religious or designs or insignia representing a movement or lobby. No visible body piercings.

- **Accessories:** Clean, conservative, professional-looking notebook, portfolio or slim briefcase (for holding unfolded resumes, notepad and writing pen). The portfolio or briefcase should coordinate with the color of your shoes. Avoid bringing a purse. No pictures promoting your favorite sports team, movie or other images on the notebook or carrying device. No backpacks or other book bags. The interviewers normally have their own copy of your resume they received from the recruiter; therefore, a simple small notebook or portfolio should do if you need to bring these things. No need to bring documents showing your previous work unless you are told to do so before the interview.

Research the Company Client

In my book *Job Hunting Ninja Master*, I go into great detail in my discussion about the different types of job recruiters, how much is their commissions and how to deal with recruiters. In that book, I write about the importance of getting from recruiters the name of the company client where the recruiter wants to submit your resume, as well as getting the company address. Once you know the name of the company, you can perform a thorough online search of the company's website in addition to other information about the company on Internet search engines, such as

Google, Yahoo! or Bing; or on social media sites, such as Facebook or LinkedIn.

Now that you have that company information, it's time to use that information to your advantage in preparation for your job interview. Review the following information on the company's website, social media and other online sites in preparation for your interview with that company:

- **Company's purpose and mission statement:** Familiarize yourself with what the US government agency or private company does for a living. If the company's home page does not provide this information, look in the *"About Us"*, *"Who We Are"* or *"What We Do"* sections of the company website.

  During your interview introductions, the person leading the interview will oftentimes tell you about their company as well as how the team you'll be on (if you get hired) fit into the company picture. However, you should always have a good understanding of the company's purpose, mission and goals before you go into the interview.

- **Company history and latest news:** Read about when, where and how the company was created; growth (in personnel, locations, acquisitions and annual revenue) over the years; and most recent news. This company information is usually found in the *"About Us"*, *"Who We Are"* or *"News & Events"* sections of the company website.

  When it's your turn to ask the recruiters questions or provide closing comments at the end of your interview, this is a good time to share what you know about the company in your closing conversation. Share your knowledge of recent news or other locations where this company operates to show the interviewers your research and interest in their company. This will make another good impression on your interviewers because it shows you were interested enough in their company to research the company.

I usually jot down some notes about the company on a piece of paper that I bring with me to the interview. At the end of the job interview, when they ask me if I have any questions, I'll reference these notes during my closing comments. In this chapter and in chapter 3, I'll show you how to incorporate this company information into your phone interview and in-person job interview.

- **Company posts and reviews:** There are other places you can look to learn about a company besides the company's own website. Today, many companies are posting their profiles on social media sites, such has LinkedIn and Facebook. If you type in the company's name using an online search engine, such as Google, Bing or Yahoo!, you can find a wealth of information about companies. There are also websites that provide reviews of companies by their employees or former employees, such as Glassdoor (glassdoor.com), Jobeehive (jobeehive.com), RateMyEmployer (ratemyemployer.ca), Kununu (kununu.com), JobAdviser (jobadviser.com.au) and TheJobCrowd (thejobcrowd.co.uk).

You can get a better picture of the company's employees, facilities, on and off campus activities, working environment and culture by viewing the posts and pictures on these sites.

Before one of my scheduled job interviews, I used a search engine to find information about the company and discovered the company was losing money and was recently acquired by another company. This company, which was once the headquarters, was now being run by another company that was downsizing their IT departments and personnel and moving their headquarters to another state. These were important events about the company that my staffing agency recruiter did not inform me about. However, I learned about these events before my interview because I had done my research on the company.

- **Company leadership:** Review the top brass—company President, Chief Executive Officer (CEO), Chief Financial Officer (CFO) and department leaders, especially leadership in your department (if you know the name of the department you could be working in). Once you are hired, you will no doubt hear these names again or possibly get a visit from them while you're at work. This information is usually found in the *"About Us"* or *"Who We Are"* sections of the company website.

- **Company address:** You can verify the company address the recruiter gave you with the address on the company website. If the company's home page does not provide the company address, look in the *"Contact Us"* section of the company website.

  If the recruiter gave you the company name but not the address, looking up the company's name with an online search engine is a good way to find the address.

  Rest assured, once you have secured an in-person interview with the company, the staffing agency recruiter or company HR rep will ensure you have the company's address.

  Having the company's address, particularly knowing what city the company is located in, will help you decide if the company's location is within your desired commute. Obviously, you want to get this information from the recruiter before the recruiter submits your resume to the hiring manager. I've refused many job opportunities from recruiters simply because I did not want to drive so far through congested traffic to the city where the job site was located.

  If you are willing to commute to where the employer's company is located, and you are asked to come in for an in-person interview, the company's address will help you determine how long it will take you to drive, take a bus, train or subway to your interview from your home on time.

- **The interviewers.** Oftentimes the staffing agency recruiter or account manager will provide the names of one, some or all of the people who will be your interviewers along with the location, date and time of your scheduled interview. If the recruiter or account manager does not provide you any names of the people interviewing you, ask the recruiter or account manager to get you the names of your interviewers.

Just as you would research the employer's company, research what you can about your interviewers on social media sites, such as Facebook or LinkedIn. This will provide you valuable information about the interviewer's technical background, work history, as well as their personal interests. This information will be extremely helpful in you establishing a rapport quickly with the interviewers by showing them you are not only interested in them enough to look them up online but that you also have common interests. However, do not try to establish rapport with your interviewers by connecting with them online, such as sending them a Facebook Friend Request or inviting them to connect with you on LinkedIn.

This information about your interviewers will allow you to connect with them while they consider your "cultural fitness" for the job. Your cultural fitness determines your ability to fit in and work well with the members of your new team. Culturally fitness involves your appearance, personality, enthusiasm, interests, sincerity and attitude that's on display while you are answering your interviewer's questions. Your cultural fitness also involves your social skills, oftentimes referred to as soft skills.

Rarely do interviewers select a candidate for the job based solely on their "technical fit". Technical fitness is your experience, knowledge and understanding of the job that's on display when you answer technical questions that relate to the job description.

Interviewers always take into account how well they think the candidate can fit in socially with their group, their team when considering the candidate for the job. This is your cultural fit.

By researching the interviewer's social media posts, you can find out what things the interviewers are interested in; their hobbies, favorite sports or sports teams; and their recreations or places they've visited or vacationed.

By bringing up things your interviewers are interested in, you enable the interviewers to see you more as someone they can connect with and get along with at work instead of just another distant "candidate" with no social connection. This social connection will help influence and convince your interviewers that you would make a good cultural fit on their team because of the things you have in common.

So when is the best time to mention things you have in common with the interviewers? Bring these things up at the beginning of your interview during the introductions when you are asked to tell the interviewers about yourself.

After the hiring manager or other person leading the phone interview or in-person job interview introduces everyone and tells you about their company, he or she will then ask you to tell them about yourself. When the interviewer says to you, "***Tell us a little bit about yourself***", the interviewer is not simply asking you to tell them about your technical background. They are actually asking you to tell them a little something about your personal background too.

Some candidates think being asked to tell the interviewers about themselves means to go through this long-winded timeline of their past job history. This is not what the hiring manager or the interviewers are looking for when they ask you to tell them about yourself.

What the interviewers are looking for are two things:

1. Your technical fit.

2. Your cultural fit.

The way you should tell the interviewers about yourself is through the lens of your technical fitness in fulfilling the requirements outlined in the job description and your cultural fitness to interact well with your new team members. This applies to both phone interviews and in-person job interviews. We'll cover your technical fit and cultural fit in greater detail later in this and the next chapter.

Research the Job Description

Another piece of information you need to get from recruiters is the job description showing the responsibilities the person in that available position will perform.

First of all, the job description will reveal if you are capable of working, or whether you even want to work, in a job with the requirements listed in the description. The description should give you enough information to make your decision on whether or not to move forward with the recruiter in submitting your resume to the employer.

Oftentimes, a recruiter will email you a small portion of the job description when they first contact you. If the description is too short for you to make an informed decision, you should ask the recruiter to send you the full job description. I've asked recruiters many times to email me a longer job description which they have done for me.

Employers Don't Expect You to Know Everything in the Job Description

Don't be intimidated by everything you see in the job description. Rarely is a person capable of knowing or doing everything in most job descriptions.

The question you should ask yourself is: *Can I do most things in the job description and would I enjoy learning the rest of the things I don't know?*

If your answer is yes, you should go for it and allow the recruiter to submit your resume to the employer.

Very few people know everything employers list in their job descriptions. Take my field in IT for example. No one knows everything about the ever-growing IT technology explosion. Someone who knows a little something about the spell-bounding exponential growth of technology is Gordon Moore. Moore's Law is named after Dr. Gordon E. Moore, the co-founder of Intel Corporation and Fairchild Semiconductor. In 1965, Moore stated that the number of components (transistors) per integrated circuit (IC) would double every year; and in 1975, he updated his prediction by saying these micro-components would double every two years. Moore was right in his observations and predictions.

In today's fast-paced growth of technology, you are not going to know every concept, device, network, application and configuration out there. Nobody is that smart, and nobody has the time, energy or money to learn everything. US government agencies and corporations know that too. What US government agencies and corporations want is someone who would be a good fit—*technically* and *culturally*—on their team; someone who knows or can do the majority—*not all*—of the items on the job description; and is willing to learn the things they don't know.

The Job Description Reveals What Subjects the Interviewers Will Ask Questions About

The second reason for asking for the job description is it reveals the subjects the employer's interviewers will be asking you questions about. The job description is like a summary or overview of the type of questions that will be on a test in school.

If you've decided to let the recruiter submit your resume for the job opening, review the job description carefully and identify areas that are your strong points; areas that you are weak in; and areas you don't know. Focus your review on areas you are familiar with first. Brush up on those subjects; reviewing and familiarizing yourself with those subjects. Once you've completed that review, research and learn as much as you can about areas in the job description that you have little or no familiarity with.

Your Resume for the Job Interview

Your Resume Review Ensures Your Interviewers Have the Latest Version of Your Resume

Before you even give the recruiter a copy of your resume to pass on to the hiring manager, you should always check your resume one last time for editing. This is your one last chance to make sure your potential interviewers see only what you want them to see in your resume. Your resume may have been sitting on online job boards for quite some time; and it may have been a while since you last looked at your resume. So give it one last look before handing it over to the recruiter.

In your interview, you will not only be tested on your knowledge and experience about the items in the job description, you may also be asked questions about items that are in your resume, such as equipment, processes, technologies, protocols, applications, certifications or previous job experience. Actually, anything you put in your resume is free game for interviewers to ask you questions about if they want to.

This should be an important reminder to you that you should only put items in your resume that you can confirm and talk about in an interview. There's nothing worse than having an interviewer point out a specific item in your resume and then start asking you questions about it when the only answer you can give them is the deer in the headlights look. So make sure you trim your resume accordingly for the job you are interviewing for.

Your Resume Review Ensures You Are Prepared to Talk About Your Resume

Sometimes, interviewers will ask you questions about certain sections of your resume. A good review of your resume before the interview will help you talk confidently about the Work History section of your resume if the interviewers ask you questions about some of your past work.

When interviewers ask you about previous jobs you worked at, use that as an opportunity to toot your own horn about yourself. I'm talking about making yourself stand out among the other candidates those interviewers plan to interview for that same job. Your next source of income is on the line in this interview, so this is not the time to be bashful, humble or shy—talk about yourself.

The proper way to toot your own horn about yourself is by using the Work History section of your resume to show the hiring manager and other interviewers reviewing your resume how your contributions at past jobs had a direct *positive impact* on the company or workplace where you worked. Just showing what actions you took, what tasks and assignments you completed or what projects you accomplished in your resume is not enough. You need to show the positive *results* and *impact* of your actions.

By "*results and impact*" I mean you need to show the hiring manager how what you did at previous workplaces saved time, energy, money; improved processes, documentation and drawings; met critical deadlines and shortened delivery times; increased productivity and revenue; satisfied customers and stakeholders; educated and trained personnel;

troubleshot and repaired critical components that restored or allowed continued service to customers and the mission; and awards, recognition and promotions received from company leadership for outstanding work. In other words, the Work History section is the area in your resume that convinces the employer that they can expect a return on their investment in you. That's what will set you apart from other candidates that have similar keywords, phrases, skill sets and qualifications in their resume as you.

By reviewing your resume for things you did at previous jobs, you will be able to more quickly and easily remember and point out the things you accomplished and how your actions produced results and positive impacts on the job.

When the interviewer asks you about past work, answer in a way that shows the interviewer how what you did at that previous workplace saved time, energy, money; improved processes, documentation and drawings; met critical deadlines and shortened delivery times; increased productivity and revenue; satisfied customers and stakeholders; educated and trained personnel; or troubleshot and repaired critical network components that restored or allowed continued service to customers and the mission.

Certification's and Experience's Place in Job Interviews

Employers are willing to pay 6-figure salaries to professionals who possess a certain amount of knowledge, skill sets and experience, and who have certain types of certifications regardless of their degrees.

This is especially true when it comes to your job interview.

Other than checking off a box for some positions requiring a degree, it is certifications that rule supreme over college degrees for many job interviews. As someone who works in the IT industry, it never ceases to amaze me how impressed and fascinated recruiters and interviewers are with the IT certifications on my resume instead of the degrees on my resume. Not once over the years have I ever had a recruiter or interviewer say to me, "*That's a really nice degree you have there*" or "*Your degree is really something to behold.*"

In many career fields, certifications trump a degree, and experience trump a degree and certifications.

Here's the difference between a degree, a certification and experience to employers:

- **A degree** just tells an employer you have the mental capacity for the job.

- **A certification** tells an employer you have the knowledge for the job.

- **Experience** tells an employer you can do the job.

It's amazing how much we invest in our education with so little return on that investment. You spend all that time, energy, money, sweat and tears over years of sitting on hard school chairs; handwriting or typing instructor notes until your fingers were numb; burning the midnight oil reading books, researching online and writing papers; buying expensive textbooks on a thin budget; taking classes on subjects you would never have taken if they weren't required; overcoming fear and trepidation while cutting your teeth on giving oral presentations; and dissecting every partition of your gray matter for answers to tests, midterms and finals.

Once that sheepskin is hanging prominently on your wall and given its proper place on your resume, what response do you get from recruiters and interviewers for all that hard work? Wait for it . . . crickets. Nada, nothing, not a peep.

What you will hear often from recruiters or interviewers is, "*I noticed you have your* [fill in the blank] *certification*" or "*Your certifications are pretty impressive.*" That's because, when it comes to many jobs, your certifications say more about your technical fit for most of these jobs than a college degree.

In addition to certifications giving you more leverage in asking for higher pay during salary negotiations, having multiple certifications on your resume will immediately get the attention of recruiters and employers.

How many certifications should you have? I say as many as your budget, time and interests will allow. The more certifications you have on your resume, the more you will stand out among your peers in the eyes of your interviewers before you even call in for a phone interview or step into that interview room.

If you completed only one or two of multiple exams required for a particular certification, include the exams you passed in your resume even though you don't have the certification yet. This shows your interviewers you are taking the initiative to improve your skills; something interviewers, bosses and employers desire in their employees.

If this information is discouraging to you right now because you have little to no certifications, don't despair. Fortunately, your interview is not based solely on your certifications, but also on your experience and skillsets you've highlighted in your resume; your ability to answer technical questions; and your cultural fit in the company.

Here's more good news for you: getting certified is not a one-time deal for one interview; it should be a continuous goal throughout your entire career. The longer you are in your career, the more certifications you should be racking up along with your experience and skills. Take the time to get certified.

Take this for what it's worth: having certifications and experience is more important than having higher or advanced degrees when it comes to many job interviews.

Angela Duckworth earned her Ph.D. at the University of Pennsylvania where she is now the associate professor of psychology. She has been an advisor to the White House, the World Bank, Fortune 500 companies and to NFL and NBA professional sports teams. In 2013, Dr. Duckworth gave a TED talk on TED.com, a nonprofit organization that shares ideas about technology, entertainment and design (TED) worldwide. Her talk was titled *Grit: The power of passion and perseverance*, and it is also the title of her 2016 New York Times Best Seller book.

Dr. Duckworth and her team conducted extensive research across all levels of academia to find out the single factor that produces success. Her study revealed that *"one characteristic emerged as a significant predictor of success; and it wasn't social intelligence, it wasn't good looks, physical health, and it wasn't IQ. It was **grit**."*

Duckworth defines grit as *"passion and perseverance for very long-term goals"*.

Because of this passion, drive and determination that Dr. Duckworth calls grit, it is also possible to have great success in life without higher education. If you think it's ludicrous to suggest you can become very successful in your career and obtain higher salaries without higher education, try convincing these following people otherwise.

Bill Gates, whose estimated net worth of $82.9 billion in 2016 made him the richest person in the world, entered Harvard University in 1973. While at Harvard, he created the Microsoft Company in 1975, and later dropped out of Harvard in 1976 at the age of 21 to focus on his company. In June 2007, 31 years after dropping out of Harvard, Bill Gates was given an honorary doctorate of Laws degree from Harvard. Gates told the crowd who witnessed his honorary degree, *"I'll be changing my job next year, and it will be nice to finally have a college degree on my resume."*

Mark Zuckerberg's high school years were spent at the Academy of Phillips Exeter, a boarding school in Exeter, New Hampshire where he graduated in 2002. In that same year he entered Harvard where he started his Facebook project and dropped out of Harvard in his sophomore year, only two years in the Ivy League, to concentrate on his Facebook social media project. Zuckerberg's 2016 estimated net worth was $51.4 billion making him the 6th richest person in the world at the time.

American businessman Larry Ellison, cofounder and CEO of Oracle Corporation studied at the University of Illinois at Urbana-Campaign for two years before dropping out of that college; and attended the University of Chicago but dropped out of that college after one term. In 1977, he founded Software Development Laboratories (SDL) with two other partners; later renamed it Relational Software Inc. in 1979; and then renamed it again to Oracle Systems Corporation in 1982. Ellison's 2016 estimated net worth was $49.5 billion making Ellison the 7th wealthiest person in the world at the time.

Entrepreneur Elon Musk, the founder of Tesla and SpaceX, started his college education at Queen's University in Canada at age 19, but in 1992 he transferred to the University of Pennsylvania where, in 1995, he earned bachelor's degrees in economics and physics at age 24. In that same year, he entered Stanford University where he planned to pursue a Ph.D. in energy physics but dropped out of Stanford two days later to launch his first company, Zip2 Corporation. Musk's 2016 estimated net worth was $11.2 billion.

Michael Dell, founder and CEO of Dell Inc., a leading seller of personal computers (PCs), entered the University of Texas in 1983 but dropped out of college in his first year at the age of 19 to focus on his new company called PC's Limited which he operated out of a condominium. His newly formed company made $6 million in sales in its first year. When he incorporated his company in 1987, he renamed it Dell

Computer Corporation and sales increased to $159 million at the end of 1988. Dell never looked back at returning to college since then. Dell's 2016 estimated net worth was $20.5 billion.

IT entrepreneur and inventor **Steve Jobs**, the cofounder and CEO of Apple Computers with Steve Wozniak and cofounder and CEO of Pixar Animation Studios, began his college education in 1971 taking a freshman English class and attending lectures at Stanford while still a senior at his Homestead High School. Jobs entered Reed College in Portland, Oregon in 1972 but due to lack of funds by his parents who were paying for his education, Jobs dropped out of college after only six months. In 1976 at the age of 21, Jobs started Apple Computer with Wozniak in Jobs' family garage. At the time of his death in 2011, Steve Jobs' net worth was roughly $10.2 billion.

Besides having brilliant minds who chose to pursue their passion instead of higher education, the one common denominator in this previous list of some of the most successful and wealthiest people in the world are that they are all college dropouts; and only Elon Musk earned a bachelor's degree; while Bill Gates was given an honorary degree.

In his commencement speech to the 2005 graduating class at Stanford, Steve Jobs said, "*Your time is limited, so don't waste it living someone else's life. Don't be trapped by the dogma, which is living with the results of other people's thinking. Don't let the noise of other's opinions drown out your own inner voice. And most important, have the courage to follow your heart and intuition. They somehow already know what you truly want to become. Everything else is secondary.*"

Steve Jobs told his audience that by dropping out of college, he could stop taking the required classes that he was not interested in. It freed him to take only classes that piqued his interest. In his final words to this 2005 graduating class at Stanford, Jobs encouraged them to "***Stay hungry, stay foolish.***"

Are you trapped in the dogma of intellectuals, listening to the results of other people who say you must have a master's degree or Ph.D. to become successful in your career or make a 6-figure salary or more?

Like I said earlier, if you have the time, money, opportunity and interest in taking higher education classes, many of which are required courses you know you have absolutely no interest in studying like Steve Jobs, go for it.

But if your time, money and opportunity are limited, and you're like many of us who simply want to follow our heart, intuition, dreams and interests like Steve Jobs, then give that your full attention and focus, even if it makes you look hungry and foolish to others. For many, the way to do that is through following your passion; gaining more experience in your chosen field; concentrating on certifications in specific areas that interest you; and putting those experience and certifications on your resume.

Education's Place among Successful People

As I said, this is not a knock against higher education. Education has its place in society. By all means, pursue higher education if you have the time, money, opportunity and interest. But don't discount the power of pursuing your focused passion and interests through experience and certifications instead of higher college education. Many people have become quite successful in life by pursuing their passion without higher education.

Need more proof? Of course you do. So let's consider a few other people.

Success is Not Defined by Education

Perhaps you're not convinced you can be very successful in your career and make a 6-figure salary or more without higher education. You're not buying the idea that higher education is not needed for success. You feel people like Steve Jobs or Mark Zuckerberg are gifted prodigies who were destined for greatness from birth; an aberration of the normal path to success; and that the rest of us mortals in society must develop our greatness and success in life through higher education.

Then how do you explain these other "mere mortals" who gained great success and wealth in life with only a bachelor's degree?

- Donald Trump (Bachelor's in Economics)
- Barbara Walters (Bachelor's in English)
- Oprah Winfrey (Bachelor's in Speech and Drama)
- Conan O'Brien (Bachelor's in American History and Literature)
- David Letterman (Bachelor's in Broadcasting)
- George Lucas (Bachelors of Fine Arts)
- J.K. Rowling (Bachelor's in French and Classical Studies)
- Jay Leno (Bachelor's in Speech Therapy)
- Jerry Springer (Bachelor's in Political Science)
- Katie Couric (Bachelor's in English)
- Martha Stewart (Bachelor's in History and Architectural History)
- Stephen King (Bachelor's in English)

Successful People without a College Degree

Let's not forget our short list of successful and wealthy people who either **did not attend college** or **dropped out of high school or college** or **have no degree at all**. You could say these people graduated from the school of hard knocks with honors.

- **Amancio Ortega:** A Spanish businessman and founder and chairman of Inditex, a multinational clothing company with multiple stores such as Zara, Massimo Dutti, Bershka, Oysho, Pull and Bear, Stradivarius and Uterque. His 2016 estimated net worth was $73.1 billion making him the 2nd richest person in the world next to Bill Gates whose 2016 net worth was estimated at $82.9 billion. **Ortega dropped out of high school at the age of 14 and has no college education.**

- **Kemmons Wilson:** An American businessman and founder of the Holiday Inn hotel chain. His net worth at the time of his death in 2003 was estimated at $1.5 billion. **He dropped out of high school at the age of 17 and had no college education.**

- **Sean Parker:** An American entrepreneur who was the first president of Facebook and cofounded Napster, Plaxo, Causes, Airtime and Brigade. His 2016 net worth was estimated at $2.4 billion. **He has no college education.**

- **Francois Pinault:** A French businessman who owns Artemis S.A., a holding company for other companies including Gucci, Converse shoes, Puma, Samsonite luggage, Christie's auction house, Chateau Latour which is a ski resort in Vail, Colorado; and is an art collector of one of the largest contemporary art collections in the world. His 2016 net worth was estimated at $14.5 billion. **He dropped out of high school and has no college education.**

- **Haim Saban:** An Israeli and American businessman, media proprietor, investor, musician and TV, record and film producer who founded Saban Entertainment, a children's production and distribution company that produces programs such as Power Rangers. His 2016 net worth was estimated at $2.9 billion. **He has no college education.**

- **Vidal Sassoon:** A British and American businessman, hairstylist who created the Bob cut worn by famous fashion designers and film stars, and founder of Vidal Sassoon hairstyling salons and hair-care products. His net worth at the time of his death in 2012 was estimated at $150 million. **He was a high school dropout and had no college education.**

- **S. Daniel Abraham:** An American businessman and founder of Slim-Fast, a well-known line of diet products. His 2016 net worth was estimated at $2.1 billion. **He has no college education.**

- **Sheldon Adelson:** An American business magnate who is CEO and chairman of the Las Vegas Sands Corporation, and owner of two newspaper companies: Israel Hayom, an Israeli daily newspaper company and Las Vegas Review-Journal. His 2016 estimated net worth was estimated at $31.1 billion. **He dropped out of the City College of New York.**

- **Wally "Famous" Amos:** An American entrepreneur who is the creator of the Famous Amos chocolate chip cookies, and also worked for the prestigious William Morris Agency as a talent agent where he discovered Simon & Garfunkel and worked with Diana Ross, Marvin Gaye and Sam Cooke. His 2016 net worth was estimated at $20 million. **He dropped out of high school at the age of 17 and has no college education.**

- **Ray Bradbury:** An American writer of fantasy, science fiction, horror and mystery fiction who won numerous awards including a 2007 Pulitzer Citation. His net worth at the time of his death in 2012 was $30 million. **He had no college education.**

- **Jim Carrey:** An American actor, comedian, impressionist, screenwriter and producer who starred in roles in films such as *Dumb and Dumber, The Mask Ace Ventura: When Nature Calls, Batman Forever* and *How the Grinch Stole Christmas.* His 2016 net worth was estimated at $150 million. **He dropped out of high school and has no college education.**

- **Alvin Copeland:** An American entrepreneur who founded Popeyes Chicken & Biscuits fast food chain. His net worth in 2004, four years before his death in 2008, was estimated at $319 million. **He dropped out of high school and had no college education.**

- **Simon Cowell:** An English entrepreneur, film, record and TV producer and reality TV judge known for his brash but effective talent competition judging in shows such as *American Idol*, *The X Factor* and *America's Got Talent*. His 2016 net worth was estimated at $550 million. **He dropped out of school at the age of 16 after passing some General Certificate of Education (GCE) Level O courses at Dover College in the UK, a boarding school for boys and girls ages 3-18; and has no college education.** GCE Level O courses are less than GCE Level A courses which are the equivalent to a high school diploma.

- **Tom Cruise:** An American actor and filmmaker starring in roles in films such as Top *Gun*, *A Few Good Men*, *Minority Report*, *Edge of Tomorrow* and *Mission Impossible*. His 2016 net worth was estimated at $480 million. **He has no college education.**

- **Johnny Depp:** An American actor, producer and musician who starred in roles in films such as *Platoon*, *Edward Scissorhands*, *Sleepy Hollow*, *Pirates of the Caribbean* and its sequels and *Alice in Wonderland*. His acting awards include the Golden Globe Award and the Screen Actors Guild Award for Best Actor. His 2016 net worth was estimated at $400 million. **He dropped out of high school at age 15 and has no college education.**

- **Leonardo DiCaprio:** An American actor and film producer starring in roles in films such as *Titanic*, *The Man in the Iron Mask*, *Catch Me If You Can*, *The Aviator*, *The Great Gatsby* and *The Revenant* which won him the Golden Globe Award for Best Actor. His 2016 net worth was estimated at $217 million. **He dropped out of high school but later earned his GED diploma, and has no college education.**

- **Walt Disney:** An American entrepreneur, animator, voice actor and film producer well-known for his Disney films and Disney theme parks. His net worth at the time of his death in 1966 was $5 billion. **He dropped out of high school at age 16 and had no college education.**

- **Robert Downey Jr.:** An American actor starring in roles in *Chaplin* which won him the BAFTA Award for Best Actor in a Leading Role and multiple Marvel Comics films as Iron Man. His net worth was estimated at $240 million. **He dropped out of high school but later earned his GED while in prison. He has no college education.**

- **David Green:** An American businessman and founder of Hobby Lobby, the arts and crafts chain stores. His 2016 net worth was estimated at $5.8 billion. **He has no college education.**

- **Joyce Hall:** An American businessman and founder of Hallmark Cards. His net worth at the time of his death in 1982 was $1 billion. **He dropped out of grade school and had no college education.**

- **Ernest Hemingway:** An American novelist, short story writer and journalist who won the Nobel Prize in Literature. He wrote the novels *The Sun Also Rises*, *For Whom the Bells Tolls* and *The Old Man and the Sea*. His net worth at the time of his death in 1961 was estimated at $1.4 million. **He had no college education.**

- **Ingvar Kamprad**: A Swedish businessman and founder of IKEA, the popular Swedish retail furniture company. His 2016 net worth was estimated at $3.4 billion. **He has no college education.**

- **Jennifer Lawrence:** An American actress well-known for her starring roles in films such as the *X-Men* and *Hunger Games* franchises; having won an Academy Award for Best Actress, a BAFTA Award for Best Actress in a Supporting Role and three Golden Globe Awards. Her 2016 net worth was estimated at $110 million. **She has no college education.**

- **Stan Lee:** An American comic-book writer, publisher, media producer, TV host, actor and former president and chairman of the popular Marvel Comics that has been converted to the ever-popular *The Avengers, X-Men, Spider-Man, Hulk, Fantastic Four, Iron Man* and *Thor* films. His 2016 net worth was estimated at $50 million. **He has no college education.**

- **Carl Lindner Jr.:** An American businessman, founder of United Dairy Farmers, former owner of Chiquita Brands and former part owner and CEO of the Cincinnati Reds professional baseball team. His 2006 net worth prior to his death in 2011 was estimated at $2.3 billion. **He dropped out of high school and had no college education.**

- **Katy Perry:** An American singer, songwriter and actress whose album, *Teenage Dream*, earned five Number 1 *Billboard* Hot 100 songs, second only to Michael Jackson's album *Bad*, and has sold over 100 million records globally. Her 2016 net worth was estimated at $125 million. **After she completed her GED requirements at age 15, she left her high school in her freshman year and has no college education.**

- **Kelly Ripa:** An American actress, dancer and TV talk show host popularly known for hosting *Live! With Kelley*. Her 2016 net worth was estimated at $100 million. **She dropped out of Camden County College.**

- **Richard Schulze:** An American businessman and founder and former CEO and Chairman of the Best Buy electronics store chain. His 2016 net worth was estimated at $2.8 billion. **He had no college education but was given honorary doctoral degrees from the University of St. Thomas in Saint Paul, Minnesota and from the University of Minnesota.**

- **Maurice Sendak:** An American author and illustrator of children's books who wrote *Where the Wild Things Are* that sold over 19 million copies worldwide and was made into a movie, *In the Night Kitchen* and *Outside Over There*. His net worth at the time of his death in 2012 was estimated at $20 million. **He had no college education.**

- **Will Smith:** An American actor, producer, rapper and songwriter who starred in *The Fresh Prince of Bel-Air* TV sitcom and starred in roles in films, such as *Bad Boys*, *Independence Day*, *Men in Black*, *Enemy of the State*, *Wild Wild West*, *Ali* and the *Pursuit of Happyness*. His 2016 net worth was estimated at $250 million. **He has no college education.**

- **Quentin Tarantino:** An American actor and filmmaker who wrote and directed several films, such as *My Best Friend's Birthday*, *Reservoir Dogs*, *Pulp Fiction* and the *Kill Bill* franchise. He won numerous awards including two Academy Awards, two Golden Globe Awards and two BAFTA Awards. His 2016 net worth was estimated at $100 million. **He dropped out of high school and has no college education.**

- **Dave Thomas:** An American businessman and founder and CEO of the Wendy's fast-food restaurant chain. His net worth at the time of his death in 2001 was estimated at $4.2 billion. **He dropped out of high school at the age of 15 and had no college education. He later obtained his GED about 46 years after dropping out of high school.**

There is too much overwhelming evidence here to say these people are an anomaly of the required path of higher education needed to become successful and wealthy in life. These people are overwhelmingly the norm; not the exception to becoming successful in your career and making 6-figure salaries, millions or even billions of dollars. All of these people did it as a high school or college dropout or as someone without any college education at all.

This list should be good news for those of you without degrees who think you're at a disadvantage going into that job interview room because of the false notion that only a college degree will get the attention of your interviewers.

I'm not saying if you take the long-accepted traditional route of higher education, you can't become successful or wealthy in life. What I am saying is that there are more than one path to a successful career and wealth besides having a master's degree or Ph.D.

Some of you with faith in God would argue that these people made it in life because of God's blessing on their life. Being a man of faith, I agree with you. However, some people prefer to view things from a physical perspective rather than from a spiritual one. Some people need a scientific formula for the overwhelming number of people without high school and college degrees who became successful millionaires and billionaires. To those of you who need an *intellectual* answer, I would say to you that it is because of this passion, drive and determination that Dr. Duckworth calls **grit**.

Passion plus value equals success.

But passion, drive and determination without a goal that eventually becomes something of **value** to others takes you nowhere. All of these people with no high school or college educations became successful and wealthy because of their passion, drive and determination to produce things of value to other people. Albert Einstein said, *"Strive not to be a success, but rather to be of value."*

Create value to others and you create success. To many employers, experience and certifications have higher value than college degrees.

Although I purposely chose this lengthy list to prove my point, it is still nonetheless a short list compared to all the people who have accomplished great success and fortune in life without a college education or who dropped out of high school or college. I realize this list of successful people I provided was so long it made your eyes bleed. I get it—this list is long-winded. The amazing thing about this list though is that it is the **short list** version. Time would fail us if I tried to tell you about all the people with poor, struggling, difficult upbringings; or who are without college degrees or higher education that became successful, rich and famous. I wanted to share that list with you in order to share what I'm going to tell you next.

SUCCESS DOESN'T PLAY FAVORITES

Success is not prejudice or biased. Success doesn't care if you're well educated or have no education at all. Success won't pass up on you in favor of someone else because of your race, religion, gender or sexual orientation. Success doesn't consider whether you came from the ghetto or a golden palace. Success plays on an even playing field where all players—you and I—have the same opportunity to win.

This should bring great comfort and inspiration to you who feel you are at a disadvantage because of your lack of education or your background. You're not at a disadvantage; you're in that group of millionaires and billionaires who became successful without college degrees or a life handed to them on a silver platter. With so much overwhelming evidence, there's really no excuse for you if you have little or no education to not chase after your dreams like everyone else. Don't let other people talk you out of your dreams. Go after your passion—success will follow.

Arrival at Your Job Interview

When the employer invites you to come in for an in-person interview, they will provide you the address to their worksite where your interview will take place. If the staffing agency is in your local area, the staffing agency recruiter or account manager may be meeting you for the first time at the interview site too; and will introduce you to one of your interviewers who will bring you to the interview room.

One of the things you should do in your pre-interview preparation is make sure you know how to get to the interview location from your home, whether it is by car, train, subway or bus. Once you have the company address, you should take a test drive (or test ride by train or bus if that is your mode of transportation) to the interview site to see how long it will take you to get there; and if there are any roadblocks, construction or other unknowns or possible delays along the way.

Here's where you can make your first of many good impressions by ensuring you arrive several minutes early before your interview time. The key here is you want to give yourself enough time to comfortably make it to your interview on schedule with a few minutes to spare. You should arrive at the company building at least 10–15 minutes early. However, you should not announce your arrival to your interviewers until 5–10 minutes before your interview start time.

I cannot tell you how many times I drove a practice run from my home to the interview site, only to discover obstacles that would have made me late to my interview, such as traffic congestion on a busy street; the road I planned to take ended up in a hotel parking lot (sounds funny now but I would not have been laughing if this happened to me on the day of my interview); the road was blocked or under construction; or the company name had changed on the building of my interview.

Do yourself a favor and discover these surprise obstacles and delays before the day of your interview. It will ensure a stress-free commute to your interview and will start your interview day on the right foot.

Introductions in Your Job Interview

The whole purpose of your phone and in-person job interview is to show your interviewers that you are a much better choice than the other candidates they are interviewing for this job. You do that by showing you are a better *technical fit* and *cultural fit* than the other candidates.

One of the best ways to show your technical and cultural fitness for this job is right at the start of your interview in your introduction of yourself to your interviewers.

Our focus in this *Before the Interview* section on introductions will concentrate on what you will prepare to say about yourself to your panel of interviewers after the hiring manager or team lead asks you to *"Tell us a little bit about yourself."*

Most interviews consist of 3–6 people on the phone interview or in the interview room with you. There's usually one person leading the interview, such as the hiring manager or lead person on the team you will be on if you are hired. The remaining interviewers on the phone or in the room are usually members of the team you will be a part of if you are hired.

Tell us a little bit about yourself.

The person leading the interview will start things off by introducing the other interviewers in the room to you; and oftentimes will break the ice by telling you a little bit about their company. Afterward, the person leading the interview will ask you to tell them a little bit about yourself.

This introduction phase of your interview is much too important for you to talk about yourself off-the-cuff or off the top of your head. You must have a well-prepared introduction plan that you've gone over with a fine tooth comb to ensure every word you speak carries weight during your introduction.

You want to use your introduction as an opportunity to stand out from the other job-seeking candidates by incorporating certain things from past jobs (your technical fit) and your personal life (your cultural fit). By using your introduction to show how your past job experiences relate to the job description for this open position, and by sharing a few things about your off-work activities and personal life, you will already be scoring huge bonus points toward successfully completing your interview before answering a single technical question.

How to Prepare Your Introduction for Your Job Interview

You should write out what you are going to say about yourself with an emphasis on your technical and cultural fitness for this job. It's best to do this on a computer so that you can quickly and easily save, update, edit and tailor your introduction for each new job interview.

Once your introduction is well-thought-out and written down, you should begin memorizing and verbally practicing what you are going to say about yourself until you can give your introduction (without reading it) in a relaxed, normal and smooth pace. Later in this *Before the Interview* chapter, we'll cover roll-playing which is a good way to practice being in a job interview giving your introduction to your interviewers.

Technical Fitness and Cultural Fitness in Your Introduction

In the previous section on researching your interviewers, I mentioned that when one of the interviewers asks you to tell them about yourself, this is not a request for you to give them a long-winded account of your work history from beginning to end. Interviewers are looking for something specific when they ask you to tell them about yourself.

What the interviewers are looking for in your introduction are two things:

1. Your **technical fit** in their company.

2. Your **cultural fit** in their company.

The interviewer is asking you to tell them things about your skill sets that can translate to accomplishing the job description of the person they want to hire; and to tell them things about you as a person that would make you a good cultural fit on their team and in their company. Therefore, the way you should tell the interviewers about yourself is through the lens filter of your technical fitness to fulfill the job description and your cultural fitness to fit in with your new team members and the company culture.

Instead of starting out with, *"It all started when I was born in the hills of West Virginia . . ."* or *"My first job was working as a paper boy in the busy metropolis of New York City . . ."*; take what you've learned from your review of the job description and start telling the interviewers specific things you've learned or done in past jobs that relate directly to those items in the job description. This will convince your interviewers that you are a good technical fit for the job without them having to ask you technical questions. Then go on and tell them some personal things about your life—your hobbies, trips, passions or interests. Try to include things you noticed your interviewers are interested in after researching their social media profiles or just share personal things in general to make an emotional or social connection with your interviewers. This will help convince your interviewers that you will be a good cultural fit in their office.

How long should you talk about your technical and cultural fit during your introduction? You should spend about **1–2 minutes** talking about your **technical fit**; and about **15–30 seconds** to talk about your **cultural fitness** during your introduction. This is not a lot of time; so make every word count. You don't want to talk long in your introduction. A long-winded introduction only tells the interviewers that you talk too much; and they will probably pass over you for another candidate they believe won't talk their ear off at work.

How to Include Your Technical Fitness in Your Introduction

When talking about your technical fit, share how things you've done in past jobs relate to the responsibilities in this new job they are interviewing you for. For example, if the job description mentions certain pieces of equipment, tools or processes, share how you worked with those types of equipment, tools or processes in past jobs. If the job description requires knowledge and experience in certain office skills or office software, talk about past job experiences where you used those types of office skills or software. If the job description asks for a person who can operate certain machinery, heavy equipment or vehicles, share how you operated those types of equipment in previous jobs. If the job description states the need for a person who can design, engineer, implement or test certain things, talk about how you performed these duties in former positions. If the job description requires you to provide leadership, training, mentoring of junior personnel or interact with customers, talk about how you handled these types of responsibilities for previous companies.

When you talk about these things you've done in past jobs, make sure you include how what you did had an ***impactful result*** for that workplace or company, just as I explained earlier. Tell the interviewers how what you did at previous workplaces saved time, energy or money; improved processes, documentation or drawings; met critical deadlines or shortened delivery times; increased productivity or revenue; satisfied customers or stakeholders; supervised, mentored, educated or trained personnel; and troubleshot or repaired critical components that restored or allowed continued service to customers or the company mission.

Don't waste your interviewer's time talking about past job experiences that do not relate to the job description when you're sharing about yourself in your introduction. There is also no need to mention things such as your certifications or degrees because these are plainly shown in your resume. You need to use those precious couple of minutes to address your specific technical and cultural qualities that make you stand out above other job candidates interviewing for the same job as you.

How to Include Your Cultural Fitness in Your Introduction

This is where your research into each interviewer's or the company's social media posts, such as on Facebook or LinkedIn, will be invaluable. When talking about your personal life, try to include things you read about in the interviewer's and company's social network profile. You don't have to mention that you read their posts or saw their pictures engaged in those same interests. Just mention that those are some of your interests if in fact those are your hobbies or interests.

When talking about your cultural fit in their company, share your interests, hobbies, sports, places you like to visit or vacation; books you enjoy reading; music you enjoy listening to; or volunteer work you enjoy doing.

If an interviewer asks you a question, such as *"What are you passionate about?"* or *"How do you spend your free time?"* or *"What do you do for fun?"* they're actually trying to find out if you have anything in common with them—your cultural fit. I've been asked all of these questions in job interviews. So don't be surprised or put off by these types of questions. They just want to know you more as a person instead of as just another job candidate.

So why do interviewers want to hear about your personal life or interests—your cultural fit?

If they hire you, your work area, desks or cubicles are most likely going to be right next to each other at work; and they just want to know if you'll fit in well with them on a daily basis. Use your introduction as an opportunity to mention things that will give your interviewers some assurance they will enjoy working alongside you. So mention things you are interested in that they posted on their social media site, such as a hobby, a book they enjoyed reading, a movie they enjoyed watching, or a place they vacationed or visited. If you couldn't find anything about the interviewers on social media posts or if you were not given the interviewer's names; you should still mention your interests, hobbies, recreation or other off-work activities to the interviewers in your introduction.

You may consider or discount this advice as over the top with too much emphasis on "**who**" you are rather than "**what**" you can do. With all due respect to your career accomplishments, keep in mind that you're probably not the only candidate with that degree, that certification, that knowledge and experience or that skill set. There are several candidates in front of you and behind you in that interview line with similar qualifications and skill sets as you who can do the same things as you in that job. When all candidates look similar in what they can do in the eyes of the interviewers, you can be sure the interviewers are going to lean heavily on each candidate's cultural fit to determine which candidate they would most likely enjoy working with all day long.

So why not take advantage of this social media profile information and make it work to your advantage over your competition? Remember, every word in your introduction counts for or against you in your interview— use that opportunity wisely.

Job Interview Questions and Answers

Interview questions for all jobs fall into one of two areas:

1. Your **technical fitness** for the job.

2. Your **cultural fitness** for the company and your team.

The topics you see in the job description the staffing agency recruiter provides you are the areas where interviewers will be asking you technical questions. The same is true if you get the job description from the job listing on the company's website. How well you answer those technical fit questions will determine if they **hire you for the job**.

The topics you normally don't see in the job description that interviewers oftentimes ask job candidates questions about are areas concerning your cultural fitness. Cultural fit questions cover your soft skills; your ability to communicate and interact with other people; your behavior or response when working in teams or groups; your ability to take criticism, feedback or advice; how you handle difficult bosses, co-workers, customers or other pressures on the job; or how well you can problem-solve issues and provide solutions. How well you answer these cultural fit questions will determine if they **hire you for the team** you'll be on and the company you'll work for.

Notice that **technical fit** questions relate to hiring you for *the job*. **Cultural fit** questions relate to hiring you for *the team*.

Job Interview Questions about Your Technical Fitness

Obviously, the technical fitness questions that interviewers ask candidates will be different for each person's field of work and each type of job within that industry. Therefore, I won't be able to provide the answers to the technical questions that each person reading this book will encounter.

Can I let you in on a secret that most writers of books on "job interview questions and answers" don't tell you?

All the books on "job interview questions and answers" you see being sold, including this book you're reading, can only provide you questions and answers about "cultural fit" questions that interviewers ask you in phone and in-person job interviews. None of these books about interview questions and answers, whether they are providing you 10 or 101 questions and answers, are about the technical fit questions you will be asked for your particular career field. All of these books are about cultural fitness questions and answers; not technical fitness questions and answers.

I'm just being honest with you. It's not possible for any author of a book about interview questions and answers to provide you technical questions and answers for every person's career field. Look closely at each "job interview" book being sold. Are they providing you questions and answers about engineering, nursing and other health care or social services, auto mechanics, food service, teaching and other educational careers, machinery, administration, management, banking and finance, carpentry, masonry or other construction work? Of course not. None of these interview books can provide you these technical fit questions and answers for interviews for every person's line of work. They can only provide you cultural fit questions and answers.

Certainly, a few rare books on interview questions and answers my focus on a specific occupation such as a book on software programming questions and answers. This would be considered a job interview book on technical fit questions and answers specifically for programmers who are looking for work.

So what can you do about the questions and answers you need to help you pass the technical fit questions that will be asked of you in your job interview?

I suggest that after you've gone through your phone or in-person job interview; always take the time afterward to write down as many questions you can possibly remember that the interviewers asked you— both technical fit questions and cultural fit questions. You'll discover over time, after interviewing with several companies in the same line of work, that many interviewers in different companies ask the same questions. By writing these interview questions down, you'll have the best reference source to go to for technical questions when preparing for your next job interview.

Having been through numerous IT interviews over the years, I've begun to notice the similarities in the questions being asked by different interviewers at different US government agencies and private corporations. I started taking notes on these questions, such as what questions were asked; which questions I knew; and which ones I didn't know. I did this until it got to the point where I had several pages of these notes.

Whenever I had to prepare for an IT job interview, I would always go to these notes first; and afterward I would review books or online material as needed to complete my review based on the job description.

When I identified items on the job description that were new to me, I would study those areas and began anticipating technical questions that interviewers would ask me; and then I created technical questions and answers for those subjects too.

Job Interview Questions about Your Cultural Fitness

A working environment is a team environment, and employers are looking for people who will contribute to the goal of establishing and maintaining a healthy team environment; not hurt, ruin or undermine team cohesiveness and a positive working environment. Employers try to bring in people to their company that will contribute to a healthy working environment by asking cultural fit questions during the job interview process.

Over the years, I've collected a series of cultural fitness questions that interviewers have asked me in many job interviews for both US government and corporate jobs. In this section, I've made these questions and the way you should respond to these questions available to you.

These cultural fit or soft skills questions and answers cover a wide range of questions that hiring managers and other interviewers ask to give them a better understanding of how you might behave and interact with different people and situations in the workplace. Questions such as *"Who was your most difficult supervisor and why?"* or *"Explain a workplace experience with a difficult person and how did you deal with them"* are intended to help interviewers uncover your behavioral tendencies in your interpersonal relationships with co-workers under stressful or difficult situations at work. Your answers to these questions help interviewers determine your cultural fit, also referred to as your social qualities, soft skills or emotional quotient (EQ) in the workplace. In chapter 3, I'll explain in greater detail what your emotional quotient is and how it comes into play during your job interview.

Some people refer to these social qualities as *how you are wired*, but that makes it sound as if these qualities are permanently hardwired in you and cannot be changed; when in fact, these are social skills that you can develop and improve.

During your preparation for your next job interview, take the time to go over these cultural fitness questions and prepare well-thought-out answers in advance that show you can handle difficult social situations in the workplace with confidence, maturity and professionalism.

How You Should Respond to the Weakness Question

One cultural fit question that is sometimes asked in job interviews is *"What is your greatest weakness?"* Sometimes this weakness question is asked in different ways, such as *"What area do you need to improve on the most?"* or *"Name one thing about yourself that needs improving."*

This weakness question is a bit tricky to answer because you are trying to put your best foot forward in the job interview. The last thing you want to do is talk about something that places you in a negative light before your interviewers and makes you look worse than your competitors. We all want to show our better selves, not our darkest angels.

So what is a bad response to the weakness question?

The last thing you want to do is ignore preparing for this question; hoping you never encounter it in an interview; only to find yourself fumbling for an answer when you are asked to share your weakness. You should also not try to sidestep this question by telling the interviewers you can't think of any weaknesses or you don't have any weaknesses.

The interviewer is asking this question knowing full well that everyone has weaknesses and each person is aware of most of them. To deny you have weaknesses or to suggest you can't think of any weaknesses makes you appear as if you have something to hide; you didn't prepare well enough for the interview; or you are too proud or conceited to accept or acknowledge the fact that you have weaknesses just like everyone else. Avoiding this question makes you appear as someone who may not accept feedback or constructive criticism well in the workplace.

Any attempt by you to sidestep this question reveals a weakness in you in the eyes of the interviewers—something you were trying to avoid all along. Instead, why not answer this question properly on your terms in a way that makes you look good—something you are trying to do throughout your interview.

Most people who attempt to answer this question about their weaknesses try to put a positive spin on it by using false weaknesses such as, "*I'm too organized*" or "*I'm a perfectionist*" or "*I'm a workaholic*". This is an old worn-out trick that interviewers see right through as a lame attempt to make yourself look good by squeezing words, such as "organized" or "perfectionist" or "workaholic", into the picture of your weakness. Nice try, but that is a failure in answering the question properly too.

So should you just spill your guts about every nook and cranny of your dark side and worst habits to the shock and horror of everyone in the room? Of course you shouldn't. There's no need to turn your answer into a freak show, horror film or a *Saturday Night Live* skit. You also don't want to mention weaknesses that are necessary or crucial to you functioning properly in this job.

Interviewers who ask this weakness question are gauging your self-awareness; honesty and sincerity about your limitations; and your ability to overcome your weaknesses and limitations through self-improvement.

What you want to provide your interviewers is a carefully crafted answer that reveals one of your weaknesses or flaws that is not a deal-breaker in your interview; can be fixed or developed; and that you are in the process of fixing and developing that area in your life. Don't mention a weakness that you are doing absolutely nothing to fix, develop or improve, such as watching too much sports on TV. (No wait, I think that's a strength, not a weakness.)

A deal-breaker weakness is something about you that would hurt your chances of being hired. Some examples of deal-breakers are stating you don't like working with people; you can't control your temper and tell people off at work; you have a tendency to ridicule people over email; you sleep on the job; you steal supplies from work or people's lunch from the refrigerator (this one should be a crime punishable by law); you're not a morning person and you have a hard time getting up in the morning which makes you late for work at times; you don't like working overtime or unscheduled longer hours; you fart a lot at work (another crime that should be punishable by law); you are a poor speller or reader; you can't handle pressure; you tend to complain a lot at work; or you tend to freeze up and remain quiet in meetings, discussion groups or collaboration sessions.

So how do you respond to the weakness question?

Pick a weakness that is still acceptable and tolerable in the workplace that you are working on to develop and improve. Here are some examples of weaknesses you can use while showing your self-improvement efforts to fix or improve those weaknesses:

- You need more leadership skills but you are reading more about developing leadership qualities or taking leadership classes.

- You lack skill or experience in a particular area but you are studying or practicing that area more.

- You get nervous in interviews but you try to overcome these nerves by preparing and practicing interviews through role-playing and positive visualization techniques as much as possible.

- You've been late to meetings because you lose track of time at work; therefore, you try to always calendar your meetings and set reminders as soon as you're scheduled for one (every interviewer can identify with this weakness).

- You can be too frank or direct at times with your co-workers but you're studying more on proper communications skills, personality types and how to properly influence people.

- Sometimes you'll spend more time than necessary on a project because you can be too critical of your own work, leaving yourself with less time to complete the project before the suspense date; however, you're trying to learn not to waste so much time checking and rechecking things too many times and by studying time management skills.

Cultural Fitness Questions and Answers

Here are some actual questions about cultural fitness or soft skills that job interviewers may ask you. After each question, I provide insight into what the interviewers are looking for when asking each question; and some suggested answers to some of these questions. This way, you can answer each question the way you want to after you understand what the interviewer is looking for when asking the question. Keep in mind that all of these questions interviewers ask are used primarily to help them determine your cultural fit in their company.

- **Question:** Who was your most difficult supervisor and why?
- **Same Question:** Tell me about a time you had to work with a difficult person on your team.
- **Same Question:** Explain a workplace experience with a difficult customer and how did you deal with them.
- **Same Question:** Have you worked with someone you didn't like? If so, how did you handle that situation?

- **Answer:** These questions really aren't about the difficult supervisor, co-worker or customer. The interviewer is not inviting you to start bad mouthing former co-workers; play the blame game; or start throwing people under the bus, backing the bus up, and then running them over again for good measure. Step away from the gas pedal.

These conflict questions are about *you* and how *you* handle conflict, difficult people or difficult social situations in the workplace.

With these types of questions, interviewers are checking your interpersonal skills, referred to as soft skills or people skills. The interviewer is trying to gauge your habits, attitudes, tendencies, oral communications, teamwork, problem-solving skills and emotional quotient (EQ) when dealing with difficult people and social situations to determine if you are a good employee and amicable person worth selecting to work for their company.

It's important that you formulate your answer in a way that shows you can maintain a mature, professional and positive behavior in difficult social situations resulting in *positive results and outcomes*. If you had some bad bosses or co-workers in past jobs, don't ever call them bad bosses or bad co-workers. Instead say they were challenging or difficult bosses or co-workers.

The wrong way to answer this question is responding to conflict *with* conflict. You do not want to appear as the type of person who would escalate the conflict further or someone who turns into a raging Hulk at the slightest provocation.

Instead, you want to show how you can *de-escalate* conflict; how you are willing to communicate professionally during conflict; and how you're able to come to healthy positive resolutions of conflicts. Show the interviewer how you will take the high road in resolving conflicts.

Most people have had or will have some form of conflict at work. If you experienced conflict at a previous job, use one of those past experiences with conflict as an example.

Go over these three areas when talking about that workplace conflict you experienced in the past:

1. Pick a specific example of conflict you experienced at a past job. The conflict does not have to involve you directly. It could be two other people in conflict at work.

2. Talk about how **you** responded to the conflict in a professional manner. Share how your words or actions de-escalated the conflict.

3. Then share how your professional response to the conflict helped (not hurt) the situation.

If you haven't experienced conflicts in past workplaces, you can tell the interviewer that you've been fortunate to have had great bosses and co-workers to work with in your past jobs; that you and your co-workers had mutual respect for one another; and that you got along well with everyone in your former jobs.

If you can answer the conflict question in one of these ways, you will pass this question with flying colors.

- **Question:** Who was your best supervisor and why?

- **Answer:** This question really isn't about your best boss, supervisor or manager. It is about **you** and how you interact with people, particularly with workplace management and authority.

    With this question, interviewers are checking your interpersonal skills, primarily your perspective on supervision and authority that will make you a good employee and compatible to work with. It's important that you formulate your answer in a way that shows you can maintain mature, professional and positive behavior interacting with both management personnel and your peers within a workplace setting.

    Use this opportunity to show your interviewers you know how to give compliments and praise to other people in the workplace— bosses or co-workers. Feel free to talk about bosses or co-workers you enjoyed working for or working with; and give specifics about what you liked about the person. Show the interviewer that you are the type of person who speaks well of people and likes to give people pats on the back. Interviewers like this because it shows you can bring a positive attitude and positive vibes to the workplace. People who are upbeat and positive are the type of people employers like to bring into their company culture.

- **Question:** Do you prefer to work independently or on a team?

- **Answer:** There is no right or wrong answer to this question because it is good to be able to work independently and on a team.

    Stating you enjoy working independently shows you are confident in your abilities; however, if you only like working independently, this makes the interviewer think you are not a good team player.

    Stating you enjoy working in a team shows you are a team player; however, if you only like working in a team environment, this makes the interviewer think you are not confident in your own abilities to accomplish tasks on your own.

    Therefore, the safe way to answer this question is to tell the recruiter you like both. You enjoy working in a team environment, but you also enjoy work independently when the job requires you to do so. By telling the interviewer you are comfortable working both on a team and independently, you make yourself appear as a person with a broader, more dynamic and complex mix of qualities for the job.

- **Question:** Explain a workplace situation where you had to think outside the box.

- **Answer:** This question really isn't about the inside or outside of the box. It is about *you* and how well you process, manage and solve difficult or complex situations or problems. With this question, interviewers are checking your abilities in problem-solving, acting as a team player, flexibility, adaptability, creativity, innovativeness, initiative and working well under pressure.

This is another opportunity for you to stand out above other job-seeking candidates because you get to talk about a challenging issue at work that you used your problem-solving skills, creativity, innovativeness or adaptability to solve the problem. It doesn't necessarily have to be an experience where you had to think outside the box; just an experience where you had to *think*. It could be a problem that required careful thought process, insight, investigation, research and application by you to make things work in that previous job. Show how what you did provided **good results with a positive impact** to that workplace.

- **Question:** Where do you see yourself in 5 years?
- **Same Question:** What are your long-term career goals?
- **Same Question:** Where do you see yourself in the future?

- **Answer:** This question might come across as odd in an age where many professionals are ready to move on to their next job in 3 to 5 years. The important thing to recognize in this interview question is that interviewers want to know if you are interested in staying long term with their company and workplace.

It costs the company money to hire you (such as paying a hefty commission to a staffing agency), and it will cost the company money when you leave. Therefore, interviewers want to know if you will give their company some return on their investment after hiring you; or do your career goals indicate that you will potentially leave their company in the near future—1 or 3 years from now.

Hiring managers also know that candidates that seek long-term relationships with their company are more likely to be more productive workers. Any job-seeking candidates who reveal they plan to move on from their company in a couple of years are oftentimes the first to be eliminated from the selection process.

Even if you don't plan on being with that company long term, tell your interviewers you hope to be with their company long term or 5 years from now (if the interviewer asks you where you plan to be in 5 years). Remember, there may be 5–15 other applicants waiting in line to interview for the same job as you. When faced with equally qualified job candidates, interviewers are more inclined to select the candidate that will provide the greatest return on their company's investment.

It's unrealistic in the 21st century to expect any job-hunting candidate to still be with a company beyond 5 years. So you're just answering their unrealistic question and expectation with an equally unrealistic answer. The fact is you, the hiring manager or anyone else doesn't know if you'll be with that company after 1, 2 or 5 years; unless, of course, you know how to work a crystal ball. Who knows, you may like it there and decide to stay beyond 5 years.

So rather than laughing in the face of interviewers for asking this outdated question, simply pat yourself on the back for their interest in wanting you to stay with their company long term. Just play along with their silly reindeer game; take a deep breath of gratitude; and then give the interviewer the assurance they need with a positive answer that indicates you plan to give them a return on their investment. You can share other long-term goals you may have; just make sure they include their company in the long term.

When you do share other goals, make sure all of these goals show how they will make you a better worker for the company. In other words, do not share personal goals that have nothing to do with the job opening or the company. Your goals are in competition with the goals of other candidates seeking that position. Don't waste this opportunity sharing goals that don't make you appear as a better choice than other candidates.

If you have a problem with this approach to this question, just remember this one thing: You could easily be more qualified than the other candidates they will interview; but this company won't hesitate to sweep you under the rug because you suggested you will not commit to the company's ball and chain beyond 1–3 years.

Here are a couple of ways you can answer the goals question:

1. *I hope to gain further experience in this company that will allow me to excel in this position, being one of your top performers and advance in this company.*

2. *My long-term goals are to stay with this company, continue growing in knowledge and experience that will benefit me* (such as pay increases or other opportunities), *this company and this company's customers.*

- **Question:** What are you passionate about?
- **Same Question:** What do you do for fun?
- **Same Question:** How do you spend your free time?

- **Answer:** If you are hired, your work area, desk or cubicle will most likely be right next to the people who are interviewing you for that job. Because of this, the interviewers just want to know if you'll fit in well with them on a daily basis.

  Interviewers also like knowing you are not just another worker who can do the job. They want a well-rounded person with a life outside of work; that you possibly have interests outside the workplace that are similar to the interviewers' lives outside the workplace.

Here are some suggestions to make a social or emotional connection with your interviewers when answering this question:

- Share your interests, hobbies, sports, places you like to visit or vacation; books you enjoy reading; music you enjoy listening to; a talent you enjoy developing, such as painting, singing or writing; or volunteer or charitable work you enjoy doing.

- Try to include things you read about in the interviewer's and company's social network profile. This is where your research into each interviewer's or the company's social media posts, such as on Facebook or LinkedIn, will be invaluable as I previously mentioned.

- **Question:** What is your greatest weakness?
- **Same Question:** What area do you need to improve on the most?
- **Same Question:** Name one thing about yourself that needs improving.
- **Same Question:** What is one thing your previous boss, supervisor or manager would say you need to improve on?
- **Same Question:** Tell me about a time when you failed.

- **Answer:** Interviewers who ask this weakness question are gauging your self-awareness, honesty and sincerity about your limitations; and your ability to overcome your limitations through self-improvement. Since I've gone over this weakness question, we'll move on to the next question.

- **Question:** Why do you want to work here?
- **Same Question:** Why are you here?
- **Same Question:** Why are you interested in this job?
- **Same Question:** Why should we hire you?

- **Same Question:** Why do you think you will be successful at this job?

- **Answer:** Interviewers use this question to not only ask you about your interest in the open position; they are asking you about your interest in their company; and they want to know what you have to offer the company.

   Your answer to this question should include three things:

   1. What attracted you to this job.

   2. Why you chose this company to work for.

   3. What you have to offer this company.

   Share what attracted you to this job: Use the job description and what information you learned about this job online to explain what attracted you to this job. Share your interest and enthusiasm in the equipment, processes, tasks, people, services or other aspects about the job description that made you want to work there. Use this opportunity to share how you performed these same aspects of the job description at previous jobs. Interviewers want to know which candidate fits best in this open position; so make sure you take the time to show how your abilities match well with the job description.

   Don't talk about the salary, company benefits or other things that benefit you instead of the benefits you bring to their company. Don't make this about serving your needs. Make this answer about serving the needs of this company. The interviewers are going to pick the candidate who is more focused on serving their company than candidates that are more focused on how the company can serve them.

Share why you chose this company to work for: The research you performed on the company will provide you several good reasons for why you want to work for the company. This is a good opportunity to show you've done your research into the company; that you like the company culture, mission and industry; and that you're impressed with the company's accomplishments, awards and press releases.

Share what you have to offer this company: Use the job description and what information you learned about the job to explain how your knowledge, experience and skill sets fit in well with this job; how you will be able to contribute to the company to produce positive results and impacts; and how you feel or know you will be successful in this job.

- **Question:** Why did you leave your last job?
- **Same Question:** Why do you want to leave your current job?
- **Same Question:** What were your reasons for leaving your last job?
- **Same Question:** Why didn't you remain at your last position?
- **Same Question:** What was it about your last position that made you decide to move on?

- **Answer:** Interviewers know candidates seeking work are like a box of chocolates: *You never know what you're gonna get.* That's why you can expect them to ask this prying question into your reasons for leaving your current or last job. They want to know if you're as good as Milk Duds or just a dud. Are you as refreshing as sweet, cold lemonade on a hot summer day or are you just another angry, sour lemon bringing your problems to their company. Are they getting another company's finest employee or someone's worst nightmare?

Your goal when answering this question is to ensure the interviewers that you're the real deal when it comes to being a quality employee worth hiring. You want to show the interviewers that you are a stable, reliable and responsible employee.

Regardless if you didn't like your current or previous job, boss, co-workers, customers or salary; don't provide your interviewers negative reasons for leaving your job. If you tell the interviewers you are leaving or left your job because of people or money; your interviewers will automatically assume you won't like their people or salary either. **Translation:** scratch your name off their list of people they would hire. Give them positive reasons for leaving your job. Show your interviewers that you are leaving or left your job for the right reasons—not the wrong reasons. Make your answer more about moving on toward something positive rather than leaving something negative. Remember, interviewers are comparing you with other job-seeking candidates to determine which person they're going to hire. Don't give them a reason to eliminate you from the competition.

You should start your answer off by telling the interviews some positive things you like about your current or last job, and then proceed to tell them positive reasons for why you plan to leave or left that job.

Some examples of positive reasons for leaving a job include looking for a more challenging job; you are looking for a position that will allow you to develop and broaden your skills or provide you more growth potential in your career; you weren't able to utilize all of your talents in your current or previous job, so you felt it was time to move on to opportunities that allow you to contribute more to a company with your skill sets; you've outgrown your current or last position and are looking for new ways to continue growing in your career; although you enjoy your job, you need to find a job closer to your home with a shorter commute time; you were working on a 6-month or 1-year contract, and when the contract ended, you decided to take some time off to hone your skills, work on some other personal projects or hobbies, complete some certifications and take some vacation time off and do some traveling before heading back into the workforce.

By the way, whenever there are large gaps of time in between jobs, you should always try to answer this question by showing you were working on *self-improvement* during your time away from work, such as constantly reading, studying or researching areas of your career field, taking classes, developing your skills through practice, working on certifications, attending workshops, self-employment activities, volunteer work, and so forth.

You should also include the answers from the previous question about *"why you want to work at their company"*, such as sharing what attracted you to their company; why you chose their company to work for; and what you have to offer their company. Make the interviewers feel as if their company and this available position is your dream job; a much better position than your previous job.

Questions to Ask the Interviewers and Closure

Once your interview is about to conclude, the hiring manager or another person leading the interview will ask you, **"Do you have any questions for us?"** Don't take this question lightly and pass on the opportunity to ask any questions. Doing so shows your lack of preparation; lack of interest in the company; and will cause you to miss out on another opportunity to shine one last time above other competing candidates in front of your interviewers.

The entire interview process is about you making yourself stand out above all the other candidates those interviewers will evaluate; and this last part of your interview should be used for that same goal. Use this opportunity to show the interviewers that you are interested enough in their company and this job that you've done your homework—you researched their company and you've prepared your questions.

Prepare 2–3 questions ahead of time that you will ask the interviewers based on your research of the company or areas where you can contribute to their team. Ask smart, thoughtful questions that are focused on how you can contribute to the company, fulfill the job description or enhance their team. Always try to ask the interviewers open-ended questions rather than questions that can be answered with a simple yes or no.

I usually type my questions on my computer; print them out, and take them with me to my job interviews. When interviewers ask me if I have any questions for them, I'll take out this list of questions and start asking my prepared questions.

The following list is suggestions on the types of questions you can ask your interviewers (pick only 2–3 questions to ask):

- *Can you share some of the hot issues, projects or immediate needs you have going on that the candidate you hire would be used in?*

  When the interviewer tells you about projects or needs that you have experience in, continue the conversation by telling them how what you did at past jobs can help them meet those needs.

- *Some teams have established procedures and like things the way they are. Other teams see room for improving their processes. Can you tell me if your team prefers to keep things the way they are or prefers to keep improving their processes?*

  This question is a great one to ask if your resume and skill sets show you have improved processes in past jobs. If the interviewers tell you they like to improve their processes, you can quickly point out how you've done that in past jobs. If they tell you they like to keep things the way they are, you know in advance the modus operandi of their team so that when you are hired, you don't try to change things. In any case, you show the interviewers you are interested in making things better for their team.

- *Based on my resume and my responses in this interview, can my skill sets help with your projects right away?*

As the interviewers try to answer this question, this prompts them to quickly consider how your skill sets can be used to fill the current needs on their team. It also lets the interviewers know you are eager to get started with contributing on their team.

- *For the candidate you select, what are the most important things you want that candidate to accomplish their first 60 days to help your team?*

Again, this lets the interviewers know you are eager to get started with contributing on their team.

- *I've researched your company website and noticed a lot of positive things about your company, such as* [name some positive things you read on their company website]. *What do you like most about your company?*

This not only shows you are interested enough in their company to review their company website and were impressed with what you read; you also complimented them by telling them positive things you read about their company. Now they get to tell you what they like most about their company—this is a win-win question for you and the interviewers.

Just as there are questions you should ask in an interview, there are some questions you should not ask. Asking the wrong questions show you didn't do any research on the company or are more focused on what the job can do for you than what you can do for the job.

When it comes to asking interviewers questions, take some sage advice from President John F. Kennedy's Inaugural Address in Washington D.C. when he took over the helm as our nation's 35th president: *Ask not what*

your employer can do for you; ask what you can do for your employer.
(Ok, he used the word "country" instead of "employer", but you get the idea.)

Bringing up the wrong topics in the form of these questions I'm going to show you tell interviewers you did not come prepared for the interview or are more interested in yourself than in fulfilling the requirements of the job. Asking poor, shallow or selfish questions will easily turn off the interviewers and lessen your chances of being selected above other candidates.

The following list is questions you should not ask the interviewers:

- Asking a question that is answered by reading the job description. This implies you did not take the time to thoughtfully read the job description. Asking these types of questions make you look like you didn't care enough about the responsibilities of the job to read the description in detail. Get the job description from the staffing agency recruiter before your interview; then review it completely.

- Asking questions related to what the company does that is answered by reading the company's website. This implies you did not care enough about their company to do your homework and research their website.

- Anything related to money. Asking questions about salary or compensation implies you are more interested in the money than in the job.

- Anything related to company benefits, such as health or dental insurance, vacation, training and education, perks and discounts. Asking questions about benefits implies you are more interested in the company benefits than the job.

- Anything related to promotions, transfers to other teams or the possibility of working a second part-time job. These types of questions imply you aren't going to stay with their team for very long. It shows you are not 100 percent focused on this job opportunity.

- Working remotely by telecommuting from home instead of coming in to work. This question implies you don't like working with customers, colleagues or leadership; or lack the available schedule or discipline to work within your scheduled work hours.

- Questions related to drug testing; background or reference checks to get the job; the company's stance on legal use of marijuana; or company policy on Internet use or monitoring of your social network profiles. These types of questions imply there is something wrong in your life that you do not want the company to know about.

- Working hours, working late or on weekends. These types of questions imply your schedule might not fit into the working hours required for this job or you are less inclined to make sacrifices to make it to work for odd hours when the work situation requires your presence. You don't want to come off as a person who is always watching the clock at work, ready at the top or bottom of the hour to leave work for the day. Once you are hired, you will be told your working hours; and may be given the opportunity to flex your hours or work remotely from home on occasion. You may need to know if this job is a swing shift, night shift or on weekends, but try to get this information from your recruiter before the interview.

- Questions about the previous person who filled this position and why they departed. This question implies you're being nosy.

Regardless who previously filled this position and the reasons for their departure; this information is none of your business in the company's eyes.

- Questions about negative things you've read in your research of the company or negative things you may have heard somewhere. These types of questions imply you do not hold the company in high regard. Just as you are trying to put your best foot forward in the interview, so is the employer. Don't bite the hand that feeds you or step on the feet that greet you.

- Questions about who or how many people are on your team to help you accomplish the responsibilities outlined in the job description. This question implies you are not qualified enough to do the job yourself, and shows a lack of confidence in your own abilities.

Closing Statements at the End of Your Job Interview

Once the interviewers have answered your 2–3 questions at the end of your interview, take the initiative to add some closing statements to make one last good impression on the hiring manager and the other interviewers on the phone or in the room. Don't wait for the interviewers to ask you for closing statements because they won't. Just add them in the conversation immediately after the interviewers have answered your questions at the end of the interview.

There are two things you need to prepare to say in your final closing statements:

1. Thanking the interviewers.

2. Ask for the in-person interview (for phone interviews) or ask for the job (for in-person interviews).

The first thing you want to close with is thanking the interviewers for taking the time out of their busy schedules to interview you. Let them know you appreciate them giving you the opportunity to be interviewed by them. Gratitude goes a long way when it comes to your cultural fit with the interviewers.

The second thing you want to do in your closing statement is ask for the in-person interview (for phone interviews) or ask for the job (for in-person interviews). The greatest salesperson in the world will not make a single sale until they ask for the sale. The answer is always no until you ask for the sale. If you don't ask, you can't have. After everything the hiring manager has told you about the company; after all the interview questions they asked you; let the interviewers know you are still interested in the open position and you are still enthusiastic about working with them.

You could combine both the thank you and asking for the in-person interview or the job in a couple of closing sentences. You could say something simple such as the following:

For the phone interview:

I'd like to take this time to say thank you to all of you for taking time out of your busy day to interview me. I'm very interested in this job, and I would enjoy taking the next step with an in-person interview with all of you.

For the in-person interview:

I'd like to take this time to say thank you to all of you for taking time out of your busy day to interview me. I'm very interested in this job, and I would enjoy working with all of you on your team.

By simply letting the interviewers know you're interested in the job and would enjoy working with them is telling them you want the job. That's all they need to hear from you to reassure them you still want the job after being grilled by them with so many questions. They may not tell you on the spot that you'll be invited back for an in-person interview or you've got the job, but you will have made a clear impression on their minds that you want the job.

Don't say, "*I want this job*", because those words make you appear desperate and it sounds like you just want the job and don't care about working with them.

Don't ask, "*When can I start?*", because that makes you come across as arrogant and as if you blindly presume you've already beat out all the competition before all the competition has had a chance to interview.

Role-Playing Job Interviews

Role-playing the interview is an important part to interview preparation. Role-play is especially beneficial if you are new to the job interview process; haven't done an interview in a while; or always seem to be nervous or apprehensive in interviews.

Role-play exercises allow you to act out an imaginary situation that mirrors a real situation to make you feel more natural and comfortable with that situation when it is happening in real life.

Practice Role-Playing with People You Know

By role-playing job interviews with someone you know, you give yourself the opportunity to practice your interviewing skills in a friendly, safe, non-threatening, relaxed, controlled environment; gauge and assess how you actually perform in an interview; identify your strengths and weaknesses; receive critiques from trusted family members or friends helping you in the role-play; and make the necessary changes and improvements to your interviewing skills after each role-play. All of these benefits of role-playing can occur before the real interview takes place.

To perform interview role-playing, you take the role of the job candidate and one or several other people will play the role of the interviewers. Use your family members, roommates or friends to help you with this role-playing exercise. You can even use your children or younger siblings and relatives as the interviewers.

As the job-hunting candidate, start with your prepared introduction; then have the person or people playing the role of interviewers ask you questions. Have one of them end the questions and ask you if you have any questions for them. That's when you should ask your prepared questions for the interviewers. Then end the interview by thanking the interviewers for their time and let them know you want the job.

Invest in your children's future—role play.

After you've practiced this several times as the candidate, you can do something really special. If you're role-playing with young family members, such as children or young adults, reverse the roles and let your younger family members be the job candidate. By allowing younger family members experience being interviewed in the candidate role, you will be providing them with one of the most important life skills they will be using throughout their adult life. Why not get them use to the idea of interviewing for a job in a fun, safe family atmosphere. There's an old proverb that says, *"Start children off on the way they should go, and even when they are old they will not turn from it."* Proverbs 22:6 NIV

Have fun with these imaginary interviews and learn to relax, smile and enjoy role-playing the interviewing process. The more you relax and enjoy these role-playing interviews during practice, the more relaxed and comfortable you will be in actual job interviews.

Don't forget that smiling and laughing is allowed in interviews. I've smiled and laughed with interviewers in a lot of actual interviews. Smiling and laughter in an interview is usually a good sign that you and your interviewers are connecting with each other—an important aspect of cultural fitness for a job. Just don't laugh for any reason in your actual interview—that means you're crazy. However, if someone said something funny during the interview, show your lighter side by laughing appropriately if someone cracks a joke in the interview. Laughing shows your interviewers you'll be fun to work with. Don't go overboard with your laugh, such as making snorting sounds or loud vociferous noises when laughing. As with your attire and appearance, keep your laughter in moderation.

When role-playing in-person job interviews, you should select a comfortable place where you can pretend being in the interview room, such as in your dining room, living room, dorm room or any other place where there is at least two chairs and table.

When role-playing phone interviews, you can also select a comfortable place, such as in your dining room, living room, dorm room or any other comfortable and quiet place. However, since this is a phone interview you are role-playing; you should communicate using your phones with the other people joining you in this phone role-play. It's best if the other people are all in another separate room from the room you are in when talking to each other on the phone. You can even have friends or family members at separate locations on their phones if your phone has conference capability.

After each role-play, allow your family members or friends the liberty of critiquing you and telling you what they felt you did well or not-so-good during the interview role-play. Tell them you want them to critique you so they feel comfortable telling you what they think.

Read through this entire chapter and the following chapter 3 on *During the Interview* before performing these role-playing exercises for job interviews.

The following list is some of the things you should include in your interview role-playing:

- Your initial greeting and handshake (for in-person interview) with the people you first meet in your interview. (This is covered in chapter 3.)

- Your entrance into the interview room and taking your seat (for in-person interview). Most in-person job interviews are in a small meeting room with a table and chairs. The job candidate usually sits on one end of the table and the interviewers sit side by side on the opposite side of the table. If you don't have a table in the room you are practicing in, that's fine. Just use chairs and sit opposite of each other.

- Your posture and attitude when standing or sitting. (This is covered in chapter 3.)

- Listening to the hiring manager introduce the interviewers and sharing about his or her company. Since this about you and not the interviewers, give the person role-playing as the interviewer a ready-made sheet they can use to introduce their imaginary interviewers and talk about their imaginary company. (This is covered in more detail in chapter 3.)

- Share some things about yourself—your technical fit and cultural fit—when the interviewer asks you to tell them about yourself after their interviewer introductions. **1–2 minutes** talking about your **technical fit** and about **15–30 seconds** to talk about your **cultural fitness**.

- Answering questions from the interviewer/s. Use a checklist of technical and cultural fit questions the role-playing interviewer can ask you. You can make several lists of questions if you have more than one person playing as the interviewer. If possible, try to list items that are in the job description or general items in your career field that interviewers might ask. (This is covered in more detail in chapter 3.)

- Asking some questions after the interviewer asks you if you have any questions for them at the end of the interviewer. No need to memorize these questions. You can type them up, print them out and have them with you to reference at the end of your interview.

- Thanking the interviewer/s for their time and let the interviewer/s know you are interested in the job and would enjoy interviewing with them in-person (for phone interview role-play) or working with them (for in-person interview role-play). (This is covered in chapter 3.)

- Repeat this role-playing as many times as you can until you feel comfortable and confident with your interview performance.

- Most importantly, have fun doing this. You and your family or friends helping you should enjoy these role-play exercises. The more you enjoy these exercises in practice, the more you'll enjoy these job interviews in real life.

Even the US Military Performs Job Interview Role-Playing for Their Departing Military Members

Each branch of the US military has a transition assistance program (TAP), a program mandated by Congress and implemented by the Department of Defense in partnership with the Labor Department and Veterans Affairs. TAP training helps military members that are preparing to leave the military to successfully transition back to civilian life and start a new career.

Part of the TAP program are employment workshops provided by the Department of Labor that teaches departing military members valuable lessons on how to be competitive in the job market; covering topics such as employment, training and education opportunities, resume writing, job search strategies, goal setting, interview preparation, negotiating their salary and other job-hunting skills. This training gives our military members the best chance for success in civilian jobs.

When I was in the US Air Force serving my last tour of duty at Ramstein Air Base in Germany, the time had come for me to prepare to retire from the military and return to civilian life. To help prepare me for my transition, I went through the Air Force TAP program.

One of the most beneficial TAP workshops I enjoyed taking part in was the job interview role-playing workshop. This workshop split all of us military participants in groups of two. One person would play the part of the interviewer and the other person was the job-seeking candidate.

After we received lessons from our job counselors on interview best practices, we each took turns interviewing the other person as if we were the employer; and then we would reverse roles and would take a turn at being the job candidate who was being interviewed. Each time we completed our interviews, we and our instructors would provide feedback to each other about our performance as a job candidate.

At first, all of us felt a bit nervous and apprehensive as we went through the role of the job candidate being interviewed. As we repeated this role-playing, we each got more comfortable and confident with talking to our imaginary interviewer; showcasing our skill sets; incorporating our past work history in the conversation; answering interviewer questions; and highlighting how we could be a positive contribution to a company.

Thanks to those job interview role-playing sessions in that TAP workshop, I felt very comfortable and confident in interviews after leaving the military; and I've enjoyed interviewing for jobs ever since.

CHAPTER THREE

It's Game Day—The Job Interview

Be so good they can't ignore you.
Steve Martin

During the Job Interview

Everyone Gets a Little Nervous Before Game Day

It's perfectly normal to feel a little nervous before or during your job interview. Everyone feels a bit nervous before an important event in their life. Lawrence Peter Berra, better known as "Yogi" Berra, a Major League Baseball player, manager and coach for the New York Yankees was an 18-time All-Star and 10-time World Series champion while a player. When it came to being nervous, he said, "*I always got nervous the nights we played in the World Series. First pitch, I was nervous. Then after that, forget it; I'd start playing.*"

In this chapter, I'm going to show you how to forget the nerves and start playing and focusing on the game—successfully passing your job interview. I'm going to show you how to beat those nerves into submission so you can feel as confident and comfortable as possible during your job interview.

Sure it takes a little courage to speak up in that phone interview or walk in that interview room. But what is courage anyway? It is simply doing things even when you're afraid.

Mark Twain said, "*Courage is not the lack of fear. It is acting in spite of it.*"

Major League Baseball player Babe Ruth is famously known for hitting 714 home runs in his career. In 1923, he broke the record for the most

125

home runs in a season and broke the record for the highest batting average. Do you know what other record Babe Ruth broke that year? He struck out more times than any other Major League Baseball player that year. Babe Ruth struck out 1,330 times in his career; a Major League record he held for 30 years; and was known as the king of strikeouts during his career. So what did Babe Ruth have to say about striking out? He said, *"Never let the fear of striking out get in your way."*

Sure, you may strike out a few times during job interviews—so what. Everyone strikes out now and then. Don't let that get in the way of you going at bat again into another job interview and hitting a home run next time.

John Wayne said, *"Courage is being scared to death—and saddling up anyway."*

I'm going to show you how to saddle up, *pilgrim*. We all have to do things that sometimes make us nervous or afraid. The good news is that the more we prepare, practice and do those things; the easier and less fearful those things become.

The Job Interview Process

Not all employers interview their candidates the same way before making a selection on which candidate to hire. One employer may hire a candidate after one in-person interview. Another employer may choose to have two in-person interviews. A third employer may opt to perform phone interviews first as a screening process to decide which candidates they will ask in for an in-person interview. A fourth employer might screen their candidates with written technical questions first, to determine which candidates they will grant a phone or in-person interview.

Most interviews last an average of one hour from the time your scheduled interview starts to the end of your interview when you are saying your goodbyes over the phone or when the hiring manager is walking you back to the front entrance of the company building. For starting positions at fast food restaurants or some retail stores, your interview may last only 30 minutes. If your interview goes past one hour, it is usually a good sign that the interviewers are interested in you. A much shorter than normal interview is usually an indication that things are not going so well. When the person leading the interview purposely cuts the interview short, it is because he or she came to the conclusion early in the interview that you are not a good fit—technically or culturally—for the position.

Any time there is more than one interview in the interview process, it is a good sign each time you are invited back for the next interview. Take a moment to pat yourself on the back for a successful performance each time you are invited back by the employer for the next level of the interview process. It's not a time to worry; it's a time to feel good about how you did in the previous interview.

Your ultimate goal during your job interview is to show and convince all the interviewers on the phone or in the interview room, especially the hiring manager, that you are the best fit—*technically* and *culturally*—for their company and team members, many of whom are interviewing you over the phone or in that room.

By **"technically fit"** I mean you have to answer the interviewer's technical questions well enough to convince them you have the hard skills to do this job well. Your technical fitness determines how well you fit with the responsibilities outlined in the job description.

By **"culturally fit"** I mean your appearance, personality, enthusiasm, interest, sincerity and attitude you display while answering the interviewer's questions has to convince them you can fit in and work well with the members of your new team with your soft skills.

Hard skills define your level of technical ability to perform the job. Soft skills define your level of social skills to fit in and interact with your co-workers, managers and customers.

Measuring your cultural fitness does not mean that the moment you enter the interview room, someone is going to hand you a personality test to complete. What this does mean is that while the interviewers are openly observing your hard skills as they ask you technical questions related to the job description, they are silently observing your soft skills; your cultural fitness as they listen how you sound on the phone or watch how you appear in their eyes; and how you respond to their soft skills questions.

This means that your technical fit (hard skills) is observed **objectively and unbiased** by the interviewers—you either know the answers to the technical questions or you don't. The interviewer's personal feelings, emotions and opinions do not come into play in your answers to their technical questions.

Your cultural fitness (soft skills), on the other hand, are observed **subjectively and biased** by the interviewers—their opinion of you is based on their own individual perspective of what makes a person a good fit in their workplace. The interviewer's sense or judgement of your cultural fitness is based on their personal feelings, emotions and opinions.

The good news about the job interview process is that you may not be the best technically fit candidate for the job (other candidates may answer the technical questions better than you), but if you showed a much better cultural fit for the job (you made the interviewers feel they would get along better with you than with the other candidates), interviewers may be more likely to pick you than the other candidates.

The bad news about the job interview process is you may be the best technically fit candidate for the job (you may have answered all the technical questions better than all the other candidates), but because you weren't the most culturally fit person for the job (you made the interviewers feel they would not get along better with you than with the other candidates), the interviewers are more likely to pass on you for another candidate.

Your qualifications and skill sets—your technical fit—are what got you the attention of the Applicant Tracking System (ATS) recruiters use to find your resume on job sites, the attention of recruiters and the hiring manager; and ultimately got you the job interview. But your social skills, your soft skills, your cultural fit is what may be the deciding factor in getting you hired for the job.

The interviewers need to be pleased with what you know about the job, but they also need to like who you are as a person in order to select you for the job above the other candidates. Your task during the job interview process is to make them like you both as a professional who can do the job and as a person they would enjoy working with. My job is to help you accomplish both with the information provided in this chapter.

The list below is the key areas you should focus on *during* your job interview:

- Prescreening questions and answers before the job interview

- The phone interview

- Arrival at your job interview

- Introductions in your job interview

- Intelligence quotient (IQ) versus emotional quotient (EQ) for job interviews

- The importance of attitude in your job interview

- Power posture, power thoughts and power words for job interviews

- Other factors that impact your job interview

- Job interview questions and answers

- Questions to ask the interviewers and closure

Prescreening Questions and Answers before the Job Interview

In some rare instances, an employer will screen candidates with technical questions before granting them a phone interview or in-person interview. Employers may use this pre-interview screening process for senior level positions that require a greater depth of knowledge or experience, or they may require candidates at all levels undergo this prescreening process.

Employers use the prescreening process to filter out job-hunting candidates whose resume caught their eye; but the interviewers do not want to waste their time interviewing someone who cannot demonstrate the right level of technical fit they're looking for in candidates. They only want to interview candidates that exhibit a certain level of knowledge and understanding about the different aspects of the job description they want the candidates to possess. Those candidates who answer the prescreening technical questions well are given either a phone interview or in-person interview as the next step, depending on the interviewing process used by the employer.

Employers typically implement this prescreening process in one of two ways:

1. They have the staffing agency recruiter ask you the prescreening questions over the phone.

2. They have the recruiter email you the questions to complete on your own time.

The good thing about prescreening questions—over the phone or email—from the employer is that these questions give you a sense of the type of questions the interviewers plan to ask you in the actual phone interview or in-person interview. If you pass the prescreening questions and the hiring manager wants to interview you; pat yourself on the back because this typically means you have the right technical knowledge to perform well in the actual job interview.

During one job-hunting occasion for a particular IT position I was seeking through a staffing agency, the employer sent me six prescreening questions through my staffing agency recruiter. One question was on Spanning Tree Protocol (STP) and the other five questions were about routing protocols. Most of these questions were accompanied with network drawings having problems I had to decipher and fix before I could properly answer the questions correctly. This is just one example of how prescreening question can be used by employers. Naturally, the employer will tailor these prescreening questions to each person's line of work.

When the Recruiter Asks You the Prescreening Questions

When the recruiter asks you prescreening questions on behalf of the employer, the recruiter may start asking you these questions without warning in your first phone conversation with the recruiter. If this happens to you, the first thing you need to realize is the fact that you are actually being prescreened for an interview with the employer. Therefore, how you respond to the recruiter is crucial at this point.

This unannounced prescreening could easily catch you off guard because you may want to review some subjects before being asked these all-important technical questions.

You can do one of two things in response to these unannounced technical questions from the recruiter:

1. Delay the prescreening for another day.

2. Start answering the prescreening questions on the spot.

Delay the Prescreening for another Day

One option is you can tell the recruiter that you didn't know they were going to ask you some prescreening questions; and you prefer to have a day or two to go over some of your notes before you are prescreened with these questions. Don't be shy about interrupting the recruiter in the middle of them asking you these prescreening questions to tell them you want to postpone any prescreening questions until later.

If you try to answer these questions immediately over the phone and perform poorly, that will end your chances to be interviewed by the employer and you will not hear from that recruiter again—at least not for that job opening.

If you tell the recruiter you want to postpone the questions until you've had a chance to perform a quick review to brush up on some topics, the recruiter will either accept your request and contact you later or try to press you to answer those questions now.

Rarely will the recruiter pass over you and move on to another candidate when you ask to postpone the prescreening questions. Once the recruiter has contacted you, it means the computerized ATS system and the recruiter think your resume is a good fit for the job opening; so the recruiter is not going to walk away from you so easily. That would be like throwing money away, or in recruiter terms, throwing their commission away.

You are only going to have one shot at these prescreening questions. Instead of worrying about what the recruiter might think of you asking them to wait a couple of days for you to answer those prescreening questions, you should be focused more on passing these technical questions that will result in you getting that invitation from the employer for a phone or in-person interview. So if you need to postpone the prescreening questions a couple of days to brush up on some of the items in the job description, tell the recruiter to hold off on the questions a couple of days.

If you haven't even seen the job description from the recruiter yet, ask the recruiter to send you a copy of the job description first before answering the prescreening questions. No doubt, the prescreening questions will cover areas listed in the job description.

Start Answering the Prescreening Questions on the Spot

The second option is you can accept this unexpected challenge on the spot and start answering these prescreening questions off-the-cuff based on your experience, comfort level and confidence in answering these types of technical questions.

I've responded with both of these options at different times in the past when being prescreened over the phone by recruiters who unexpectedly started asking me technical questions. It just depends on how well prepared you are at the time for these prescreening technical questions from recruiters.

When the Recruiter Emails You the Prescreening Questions

In other instances, the staffing agency recruiter or account manager could email you the employer's prescreening questions. When an employer wants to screen candidates this way, the good news is that it is like taking an open book test in school. You can take your time answering these technical questions, reading or researching information found online or in your own books or notes to answer the questions. There's typically no time limit set to complete these questions, but you should complete them as expeditiously as possible.

When you are done answering the technical questions, you will email your answers back to the staffing agent who will forward your answers to the employer for review. If the employer is pleased with your answers and wants to interview you, the recruiter will let you know and ask you when the best day and time is for you to be interviewed by the employer.

Sometimes, it may take over a week before the recruiter provides you feedback from the employer because someone on the interview team who is reviewing your answers may be preoccupied with other work-related priorities or the hiring manager may be on a business or personal trip. If you do not hear back from the recruiter after 1–2 weeks, you should either call or email the recruiter for feedback. Otherwise, accept the recruiter's silence as the recruiter's unprofessional way of letting you know that the employer does not want to interview you.

The Phone Interview

The phone interview we are discussing in this section is not the phone conversations you will have with a staffing agency recruiter or account manager about a job. The phone interview *is* the job interview you have with the hiring manager and other interviewers over the phone.

After the staffing agency or company HR department forwards your resume over to the hiring manager, it is the hiring manager who makes the final decision if he and his team will interview you by either phone or in-person.

Phone interviews are an elimination process.

The phone interview is oftentimes a vetting, prescreening and elimination process that interviewers use to determine which job-hunting candidates they want to bring in for an in-person interview. Companies save time, money and other resources by performing phone interviews instead of using in-person interviews first. This is especially true when employers receive a large number of resumes of candidates that interest them. If the employer is inviting you to a phone interview, it doesn't mean the employer intends to **hire you**. Sure, the employer is interested in you based on your resume, but the employer is using the phone interview to determine if they should **eliminate you** from their list of job-seeking candidates they want to invite to an in-person interview.

There are other rare instances where the phone interview may be used as the primary means for hiring someone for the job. For instance, when I was living in Illinois, I went through a phone interview for a job that was located in Colorado. My goal was to find a job in Colorado first, and then move to that state once I was hired. The interviewers knew I was living in another state and that I was willing to relocate if I was hired; therefore, their phone interview was used in place of an in-person interview. I passed the phone interview, they hired me for the job, and I moved to Colorado.

How did I convince the hiring manager to hire me for the job with just a phone interview? By saying and doing the things I'm teaching you in this book.

Make no mistake about it: the phone interview is equally important as an in-person interview because you only get one shot at the phone interview just as with most in-person interviews.

Your ultimate goal in the phone interview is to impress your interviewers enough to make them want to invite you in for an in-person interview. Impressing your interviewers is typically an easier thing to do when you can physically meet and speak with them; display positive aspects of your personality, presence and appearance; and make good impressions with your eye contact, show of interest and enthusiasm; or other physical, social or emotional connections you can make when you are actually in the interview room with your interviewers. A phone call limits your ability to do these sorts of things. If you do not impress your interviewers over the phone, they will pass over you and that will be the end of any further chances you have of being interviewed in-person with them or being hired for that job.

If you do not pass your phone interview, it will do you no good to try to resubmit your resume to the same employer again through another recruiting agency or through the company's career website. The hiring manager and the rest of the interviewing team have already seen your resume; so they will know it is you again; and they will toss your resume in the trash.

If you pass your phone interview, you will be notified by your staffing agency recruiter or account manager that the hiring manager liked you and wants you to come in for an in-person interview. Passing the phone interview does not necessarily mean you will be hired for the job. It means that you now stand a better chance of being hired because you impressed your interviewers enough during this first elimination round to make them want to interview you in person. You should accept this as a big boost of confidence that the interviewers liked what they heard from you over the phone from both a technical fit and cultural fit standpoint.

Stay on top of your game because you are still competing against other candidates for this job that the employer has already interviewed or plans to interview after you.

Although it is only a phone interview, you should still follow all the applicable guidelines I've pointed out in the previous *Before the Interview* chapter and will go over with you in this *During the Interview* chapter. Don't wait until after a successful phone interview to learn and follow these tips, advice and procedures outlined in these chapters on interview preparation.

How Phone Interviews Benefit the Interviewers

Phone interview conference calls allow the interviewers to either gather together in a company conference room or sit at their separate desks at work while they interview you. A phone interview also allows interviewers in different locations across the country to interview you along with the local interviewers.

If interviewers gather together in a private conference room to interview you over the phone, they will receive your call over the open phone speakers so everyone in the room can hear you speak.

If interviewers are at their individual desks while interviewing you over the phone, each of them typically wear their phone headsets to hear you speak and to ask you questions. This way, everyone in the office does not hear you interviewing for the job; and gives interviewers the opportunity to sit comfortably at their desk while they join in your phone interview

How Phone Interviews Benefit Job-Hunting Candidates

Phone interviews can also be advantageous to you as the job-hunter as well. A phone interview can be a better option than an in-person interview during times when you are job-hunting while still employed in another job. If you are not working, a phone interview also means you don't have to get dressed up or drive to the interview location.

I know there are those who advocate getting dressed up for a phone interview at home. I prefer wearing whatever makes you feel comfortable yet confident and powerful. If your favorite T-shirt and jeans are what makes you feel comfortable, confident and powerful, then wear that during your phone interview at home. If wearing a 3-piece suit or business dress outfit makes you feel comfortable, confident and powerful, then by all means, wear that during your phone interview.

Phone interviews allow you to interview for jobs during working hours. I've interviewed for jobs while employed by stepping outside of my workplace and going to the privacy of my car to interview for jobs. During a break at work, I've also gotten in my car; drove to a quiet secluded location; and then called in for a phone interview.

If you will be interviewed over the phone, pick a location where you can be alone that is quiet and free from distraction. The optimum location for you may be in a room in your home, in your car or some other private area.

If you are doing a phone interview at home, take advantage of standing or sitting in a power position that makes you feel strong and confident. I'll go over both standing and sitting power positions in greater detail later in this chapter. The key here is to place yourself in a comfortable and confident physical position and mental frame of mind that will give your interviewers a better impression of you from your positive attitude, voice tones, the way you speak and the answers you give to their questions.

The advice and exercises I recommended in chapter 2 that will prepare you for an in-person interview applies just as well to phone interviews because the interviewers, introductions and questions you'll experience in a phone interview will be the same as in an in-person interview. Only difference being you and your interviewers won't be able to see each other while you are being interviewed.

A phone interview also provides you the unique advantage of having your computer, resume and notes in front of you while talking to your interviewers over the phone; something I always do when I'm being interviewed over the phone at home. Take advantage of this phone interview by having your resume, pen and blank paper, notes, drawings and diagrams, cheat sheets, lucky rabbit's foot, chicken bones or whatever else you need to have with you to help you and give you support during the phone interview.

Sometimes when I'm interviewing by phone at home, I'll have all of my notes spread out on my bed while standing confidently in a power position next to my bed where I can quickly glance at or reach for notes on a particular subject while being interviewed. A standing position also relieves pressure from your diaphragm, giving your voice more resonance and energy when you speak. This way you'll sound more confident and enthusiastic about the job to your interviewers.

It is also alright to pace a little bit while standing during your phone interview, especially if you're the fidgety type or you get nervous or feel too much energy building up during the interview. Pacing helps to work off that energy to calm your nerves. However, don't pace so much that you sound out of breath or are breathing heavily while talking to your interviewers. The goal is to relax while sounding confident, energetic and enthusiastic about this job opportunity during your phone interview.

During other phone interviews at home, I'll sit in a confident and comfortable position at my desk, having my computer at my disposal along with notes on my desk. However, it is important that you sit upright instead of leaning back in your chair during your interview because sitting upright is a power position that gives you more confidence. I'll go over the sitting power position in more detail later in this chapter. I use my computer to have the company's information up on the screen at my disposal along with other websites pertinent to the job description or subjects I think the interviewers might ask me.

Can You Hear Me Now?

Ever have your phone lose its signal strength or worse, have the battery run out? Of course you have. We hate it every time it happens because it always seems to happen at the most inconvenient time. If it happens during a phone interview, it could cost you a job opportunity. Having a phone signal that causes your voice or the interviewer's voices to crack or drop in and out does not bode well for you in this elimination process. Don't gamble away your chances of a potential in-person job interview because of a mobile phone mishap. Make sure you're in a good area where you have a strong phone signal and ensure your phone's battery is fully charged before the phone interview. As an added precaution, you can keep your phone plugged into its charger while talking to your interviewers but a fully charged phone should easily last the duration of the phone interview.

You may prefer wearing a Bluetooth headset or earbuds so your hands are free to access your computer, handle your notes or simply to allow you to pace the floor while interviewing. Make sure the person on the other end of your Bluetooth device can hear you clearly. You can easily test your Bluetooth device by calling a friend and asking them how your voice sounds to them. Do not use the speakerphone on your phone because it will not produce the same sound quality as non-speakerphone voice to the listeners on the other end. You want to put your best foot forward; or in this case, your best voice forward during your phone interview.

What's Good for the Goose is Good for the Gander

Most of what you'll learn to do in an in-person interview in chapter 2 and this chapter will apply to a phone interview as well. The same holds true for things you should not do in a phone interview that you normally would not do in an in-person interview.

The following list is some things you should avoid during a phone interview:

- **Drinking or sipping liquids.** Try to get that glass of water or drink of coffee or sip of soothing chamomile tea before your phone interview. Get that drink well before your phone interview to ensure you don't have to run to the bathroom afterward. You may need a glass of water handy only for times where you feel you are getting a case of the dry mouth during the phone interview because of nerves. If you plan to have a glass of water or some other beverage nearby, make sure there is no ice or a spoon in the glass that can be heard when you take a drink. Keep in mind that drinking and sipping sounds are a lot louder than you think to the listener on the other end of the phone.

- **Eating food or snacks or chewing gum.** Step away from the snacks. Make sure you've had something to eat well before your phone interview.

- **Starting or ending your sentences with "um", "er" or "uh".** These vocalized pauses show a lack of good communications skills and make you appear unprofessional. To listeners on the other end of the phone, these vocal pauses sound more pronounced and annoying. If you're one of those people who have to always speak with these vocalized pauses, you should use the role-playing techniques I mentioned in the previous chapter to practice answering interview questions without those pesky vocalized pauses. Instead of sitting with a friend or family member in a room, you can role-play over the phone to practice good communications during a phone interview.

- **Background noise.** Turn off any music or the TV and find a place free from other noises to keep your "remote interview space" in check. A phone is also an amplifier device that can oftentimes pick up background noise even when you think that noise level is low enough. As much as we love our family members of the two-legged and four-legged kind, the phone interview is too important to allow yourself to be interrupted or distracted. Make sure you're in a place free from noises that may be picked up by interviewers on the other end.

- **Speaking too long.** Most interview questions can be answered in less than 30 seconds. If you are taking more than one minute to answer questions that were meant to be answered in 30 seconds or less, you will come off as a long-winded person who talks too much. No interviewer is going to want to work with a person like that. Keep your answers and comments short if you want to be invited back for an in-person interview. The only time you should take 2–3 minutes to speak is during your introduction. When it comes to speaking in phone interviews, less is more.

- **Interrupting or poor listening.** Most good communications skills you use in person apply to phone communications. Never interrupt someone else who is speaking on the phone. Listen carefully to the person talking to understand clearly what they are saying or asking. If you did not understand the question because the question was not clear to you, let the interviewer know. They will always try to rephrase the question while trying not to give away the answer. If one of the interviewers crack a joke, it's ok to laugh; but don't laugh too loud into the phone. Show them you have a humorous side to you too—this helps with convincing them you are a good cultural fit for their team. However, avoid cracking jokes yourself; let the interviewers introduce humor into the conversation.

- **Typing on your keyboard or flipping through your notes or other papers.** Interviewers know the phone interview allows you to have a computer, notes and cheat sheets in front of you.

However, if they hear you searching for the answers to their questions by clicking away at your keyboard or flipping through pages, you're giving the interviewers one more reason to eliminate you from their invitation to an in-person interview. You want to make the interviewers think you can answer their questions without having to search to the end of the Internet for the answer.

How to Call In for a Phone Interview

If the hiring manager wants to interview you by phone, the staffing agency recruiter or account manager will provide you the conference call phone number and a passcode number to call on the day and time of your scheduled interview. The conference call phone recording will tell you when to use the passcode number on your phone.

Just as with arriving early for an in-person interview, you should call the interviewer's number 2–5 minutes before your scheduled interview time. Calling in late for a phone interview is just as bad as arriving late to an in-person interview. It reflects poorly on your ability to plan ahead and perform tasks in a punctual manner.

Once you are on the conference call, the phone system will tell you how many people are currently on the conference call. You should introduce yourself by stating your full name, such as *"Frank McClain is on the line"*, so that if one of the interviewers are already on the line, they'll know you have called in.

If you are the first person on the conference call, wait patiently for someone to arrive. Once you hear someone on the line, again state your full name to let them know you, the job candidate, are on the line for the job interview. One of the interviewers on the conference call will let you know if they are still waiting for other interviewers to call in.

Once all the interviewers have called in to the conference call, the hiring manager or team lead will start things off with introductions just as in an in-person interview; and everything will continue to the end of your interview as it normally would during an in-person interview. In the remainder of this chapter, I'll go over in detail how the in-person job interview process will flow from beginning to end and how you should conduct yourself throughout the entire process.

How to End the Phone Interview

In an in-person job interview, you always want to thank the interviewers for the interview opportunity and ask them for the job at the end of the interview (I'll show you exactly how to do this at the end of this chapter). However, a phone interview is an elimination process by the interviewers to determine which candidates they will allow and refuse an in-person job interview. Therefore, the appropriate thing to ask for at the end of a phone interview is an opportunity to interview in person. At the end of the interview, let the interviewers know you're still interested in this job. Then let them know you want to come in to be interviewed in person.

At the end of your phone interview, you could say something simple such as, *"I'd like to take this time to say thank you to all of you for taking time out of your busy day to interview me. I'm very interested in this job, and I would enjoy having the opportunity for an in-person interview with all of you."*

Arrival at Your Job Interview

It's Game Time!

Arrive early to your in-person job interview but not too early; no more than 5–10 minutes early. If you let your interviewers know you've arrived 15 minutes or earlier before your interview start time, they will most likely feel inconvenienced rather than impressed by your "too early" arrival. They're most likely trying to wrap things up with what they're doing at work before your arrival; and now that you've arrived sooner than expected, they'll either feel uncomfortable about making you wait longer or will have to stop what they're doing and come out to greet you.

Either way, it won't start your interview on the right foot like you thought by arriving too early.

It's good to get to the company building 10–15 minutes earlier to make sure you get there in time, but you can wait in your car until 5–10 minutes before your interview start time so that you don't announce your arrival too early to your interviewers. Turn your cell phone off, including the vibrate mode; or better yet, leave your phone in the car prior to entering the employer's building. One of the worst impressions you can make during an interview is having your cell phone go off or the interviewers seeing you look down in a response to the vibration going off. They'll all know what that look means—it means you don't care enough about your job interview to shut off your phone.

Arriving to a Job Interview at a US Government Agency on a Military Installation

If you are going to an in-person interview for a job in a US government agency, you will interview either at the government agency or a location away from the agency's building. Some government agencies are located in areas that can be accessed by the public. Other government agencies are on military installations with restricted access to only authorized personnel.

Going to a job interview for a US government agency on a military installation presents a few challenges in both getting on the military installation as well as into the government building. Do not fret; there is a process in place to get you on the installation for your interview.

You will not be allowed to enter (walk in or drive in) most US military installations without a military ID card (active or retired military), Common Access Card (CAC) or an escort.

CAC cards are issued to active duty uniformed service personnel, Selected Reserve, DoD civilian employees and eligible contractor personnel. Once you are hired as either a US government civilian employee or contractor, you will be issued a CAC card that is valid for the length of your employment or contract.

Contractor CAC cards are distinguished by a green bar across the front of the card. This CAC card will also provide contractors limited use of other services on the military installation, such as shopping at the military shoppette store (a small convenience store) or filling your car with gas at the gas station.

If you do not have a military ID card or CAC card, someone from the government facility will have to meet you at the front entrance of the military installation to escort you in to your scheduled interview.

Most military installations have a Visitor Center outside one of their gated entrances. The Visitor Center is where you can get a temporary visitor pass to enter the military installation, but you'll need an authorized person with the proper ID credentials to sign you in to get your pass. Therefore, the Visitor Center is where you will most likely meet the person who will escort you to the government agency building where your interview will take place. These Visitor Centers usually have seating areas, restrooms and a drinking fountain while you wait for your escort.

Keep in mind that this whole escort process takes time that might make you late for the start of your interview. Therefore, find out from either the recruiter or from the interviewer (the recruiter will provide you a contact phone number for the interviewer at the government agency) what time should you meet your escort at the Visitor Center.

Introductions in Your Job Interview

When Staffing Agency Recruiters Meet You at Your Job Interview

When you arrive at the employer's building on the day of your interview, you might be greeted by your staffing agency recruiter or account manager if their staffing agency is local to the employer's building. The recruiter or account manager will let you know if they plan to meet you at the interview site. If your staffing agency recruiter or account manager is there to greet you when you arrive, that person normally remains with you until your interviewer comes out to greet you. Sometimes both the staffing agency recruiter and the account manager will be there to meet you; sometimes only one of them will be there; but most times no one from the staffing agency will be at your scheduled interview.

A meeting with staffing agency personnel at your interview is oftentimes the first time you will meet the people who helped you get that job interview at your negotiated salary rate. So use that opportunity to personally thank the staffing agent for their help in getting you that job interview.

When Staffing Agency Recruiters Do Not Meet You at Your Job Interview

If no one from the staffing agency will meet you at your scheduled interview location, the first person you will most likely meet is the person at the reception desk of the employer's building or office. Let the person at the reception desk know you have an appointment with one of the interviewers you were told would meet you.

If the person at the employer's reception desk is the first person you meet, make a good first impression by smiling and being friendly with that person. There's no need to shake the receptionist's hand but always be courteous and friendly with the receptionist. If you treat the receptionist rudely or as if they don't matter, the receptionist can let your interviewers know of your unprofessional behavior which will reflect poorly on you in their evaluation of your cultural fit for their company. Your cultural fitness in a company has to do with how you interact with and treat everyone in the company, including the receptionist.

The same holds true for the person who meets you at the Visitor Center of a military installation to escort you to your interview. This person who escorts you onto the installation is oftentimes a member of the team you will be part of if you are hired.

Your Initial Greeting at Your Job Interview

When greeting staffing agents or your interview party, extend your hand, look them in the eye, smile and give them a firm handshake. Do not give one of those soft, sheepish or wet noodle handshakes. A limp, weak grip in your handshake makes you appear weak, disinterested, insecure or negative. A firm, strong handshake makes you appear strong, confident, assertive, interested and positive.

When greeting your interviewers, smile and give them a pleasant greeting, such as "*Hi, I'm* [state your first name only]. *It's nice to meet you.*"

In your job interview, different types of personnel could be in that room with you, such as a hiring manager, a team lead, and several team members. Typically, all of these individuals are members of the team you will be part of if you are hired. This is also the case for phone interviews.

The Hiring Manager in Your Job Interview

The hiring manager is a manager in the company who requested the position for his or her team be filled. The hiring manager is also the person who makes the final decision on which candidate will be hired for that open job. The title of "hiring manager" is only temporary until the manager hires the candidate for the job. Afterward, the hiring manager uses only their normal manager title. Depending on the size of the company, this manager could manage an entire section of teams; a small portion of teams in a section of the company; or only one team in the section.

The position the hiring manager is requesting to be filled is a position that is under the hiring manager's area of control and leadership. Therefore, although the manager puts in his or her personnel request to the company's HR department, the manager is the one who will take ownership of the recruiting process for this position while the HR department supports and assists the manager along the way. The hiring manager will work with the HR department concerning creating the job description of the available position; conducting the resume reviews and interviews; completing and finalizing the hiring, salary negotiations and job offer process; and establishing the start date of the candidate they select for the job after all the candidate interviews are completed. Since the selected candidate will become a part of the hiring manager's team, this manager has a vested interest in ensuring the right candidate for the job is selected for his or her team members. That means a person who is the best technical and cultural fit for the manager's team.

The hiring manager will most likely become your reporting manager in your section if you are hired for the job. The manager's office could be either in the same office you will be working in or located in another room or building.

The hiring manager could have strong background experience in your line of work; someone that possibly started at the level you're coming in at with this company; and worked through the ranks until they reached the management position they are in now. The hiring manager could also be a person with little to no background experience in your line of work but possesses the necessary managerial skills to be in that position.

It's possible for two managers to be in the interview room with you; a manager for full-time company employees and a manager for contractors. If this is the case in your interview, one of these managers will be your hiring manager depending on whether you are interviewing as a company employee or a contractor.

Such was the case when I was interviewing for a network engineer position for a service provider company. This service provider normally hired job-hunting candidates as contractors first for a 6 month contract. If they liked the contractor's performance after 6 months, they gave the contractor the option to either continue working as a contractor or become a full-time company employee.

If the hiring manager is present in your interview, he or she will introduce you to all the interviewers in the room. The manager will oftentimes share a little bit about their company before asking you to tell them a little bit about yourself. Once all the introductions are out of the way, the manager and the other interviewers will begin asking you technical questions. If the manager does not have a technical background, he or she will pass the interview over to the other interviewers to ask you the technical questions. Regardless if the hiring manager has a technical background or not, you can be sure the manager will be observing you to determine if you are a good cultural fit for his or her team as you are being evaluated for your technical fit.

The Team Lead in Your Job Interview

Each team of workers in US government agencies and corporations usually has a team leader, referred to as the team lead. The team lead is the person who is the technical leader on the team. This person is usually the senior person on the team you will be on if you are hired; is the driving force behind the team; and is responsible to the manager for the rest of the team members, assignments, progress and accomplishments.

The lead person will delegate work assignments from the team manager to you and the rest of the members on your team; however, the team lead is responsible to the manager for the overall success of the team's projects and assignments. Since the team lead is a technical person, the lead will oftentimes work alongside you to complete an assignment, project or goal. If the team lead attends meetings on behalf of the team, the lead will pass on or brief the team on the minutes from the meetings.

As a matter of protocol, when team members have issues to pass on or discuss with leadership, they first go through the team lead; then their team manager; and then to higher leadership.

When it is time assess and evaluate the performance of team members, the manager will seek inputs from the lead person about each team member. The lead may also fill in for the team manager's responsibilities when the manager is out of office.

It's normal to have both the hiring manager and team lead in the room with you during your interview. When the hiring manager cannot make it to your interview, the team lead usually takes over and leads the interview.

When It's Your Turn to Give Your Introduction in Your Job Interview

After the hiring manager, team lead and other interviewers introduce themselves to you, the last introduction during your job interview will be your carefully prepared introduction given to the interviewers. In chapter 2, I covered how you should prepare and practice for giving this introduction. Now it's time to put all that practice to good use. As Steve Martin said, *"Be so good they can't ignore you."*

In your introduction, remember to talk about things in your past jobs that relate to the job description (your technical fit), and mention a few things in your personal life that the other interviewers can identify with and connect with (your cultural fit).

Remember, your introduction should only be 2–2 ½ minutes long; so relax—you can do this. Nobody knows you better than you; so smile and be confident introducing to these interviewers the person you've known all your life—*you*. Introductions don't get any easier than that. And remember, it's not always the smartest person who gets the job; it's the person who is the best fit—technically and culturally—that usually gets hired.

Intelligence Quotient (IQ) versus Emotional Quotient (EQ) for Job Interviews

For those of you who think the smartest candidates are always going to trump all other candidates in a job interview and be the one who gets hired, think again. Since the 1990s, many scientists, psychologists, researchers and educators have been stating that your emotional intelligence (EI or EQ) and attitude are better predictors of your success in life, including in job interviews, than your IQ.

The Importance of Intelligence Quotient (IQ) in Job Interviews

The IQ is, at best, a rough measure of academic intelligence; the ability or capacity of a person to learn, understand and apply information and skills. The first intelligence quotient (IQ) test was invented in 1908 by French psychologist, Alfred Binet, when the French Ministry of Education, who passed a law requiring all French children attend school, needed a way to determine which students were not benefiting from regular classroom education and needed remedial instruction.

Today, there are a variety of IQ tests available; and the test content in each of these tests differs widely from one another. One IQ test may show you only pictures of blocks, circles, triangles and other shapes; another IQ test may ask you questions about words and numbers; and still another IQ test may ask you questions about pictures, words and numbers. Regardless of the test used, the results of each IQ test, called IQ scoring measured in Intelligence Interval and Cognitive Designation is pretty standard across the board regardless of which IQ test you take.

The results of your IQ test are normally compared to other people in your age group to determine your IQ score. You can take one of these IQ tests for free at many Internet websites, such as iqtest.com, free-iqtest.net, seemypersonality.com/IQ-Test, brainmetrix.com/free-iq-test and myiqtested.com.

The average IQ score among Americans is 98, with 99.5% of IQ scores falling between 60 and 140. The following list is the standard IQ scoring ranges and their corresponding cognitive designation; and the IQs of some famous and infamous people who fall within those ranges.

IQ Range to Cognitive Designation

- **1–40 = Mental disability (less than 1% of test takers)**

- **40–54 = Severely challenged (less than 1% of test takers)**

- **55–69 = Mentally challenged (2.3% of test takers)**

- **70–84 = Below average (13.6% of test takers)**

- **85–114 = Average intelligence (68% of test takers):** Andy Warhol (86), Donovan McNabb (88), Henry Lee Lucas (89), OJ Simpson (89), Dan Marino (92), George H.W. Bush (98), Howard Stern (99), Tim Tebow (104), Britney Spears (104), Brett Favre (104), Ronald Reagan (105), Charles Manson (109), Ben Roethlisberger (110), Al Franken, (110), Kobe Bryant (114), Drew Brees (116)

- **115–129 = Above average; bright (13.6% of test takers):** Peyton Manning (116), David Berkowitz (118), Troy Aikman (118), Lee Harvey Oswald (118), John F. Kennedy (119), Philip Rivers (120), John Elway (120), Gerald Ford (121), Courtney Cox (122), Dwight Eisenhower (122), John Kerry (123), George W. Bush (125), Lyndon B. Johnson (126), Steve Young (126), Tom Brady (126), Abraham Lincoln (128)

- **130–144 = Moderately gifted (2.3% of test takers):** Aaron Rodgers (130), Harry Truman (132), Jodie Foster (132), Nicole Kidman (132), Al Gore (134), Arnold Schwarzenegger (135), Bill Clinton (137), Rush Limbaugh (137), Geena Davis (140), Hillary Clinton (140), Shakira (140), Madonna (140), Steve Martin (142), Richard Nixon (143), Adolf Hitler (144), Napoleon Bonaparte (145)

- **145–159 = Highly gifted; Genius (less than 1% of test takers):** Jeffrey Dahmer (145), Hans Christian Andersen (145), Franklin D. Roosevelt (147), Jayne Mansfield (149), Bill O'Reilly (150), Carol Vorderman (154), Sharon Stone (154), Eli Manning (156), Ellen Muth (156), Sigmund Freud (156), Jimmy Carter (156)

- **160–179 = Exceptionally gifted; extraordinary genius (less than 1% of test takers):** Albert Einstein (160), Bill Gates (160), Quentin Tarantino (160), Reggie Jackson (160), Stephen Hawking (160), Dolph Lungren (160), Jill St. John (162), Charles Darwin (165), Johann Sebastian Bach (165), Ludwig Van Beethoven (165), Norman Schwarzkopf (170), Judith Polgar (170), Judy Holliday (172)

- **180 and up = Profoundly gifted; profound intellectual prowess (less than 1% of test takers):** Benjamin Netanyahu (180), John Sununu (180), Charles Dickens (180), Michelangelo (180), Galileo Galilei (185), Bobby Fisher (187), Philip Emeagwali (190), Garry Kasparov (190), Sir Isaac Newton (190), Johann Wolfgang Goethe (210), Leonardo da Vinci (220), Marilyn vos Savant (228)

So what about the importance of IQ in job interviews? To answer that question, I have to talk about the importance of emotional quotient (EQ) in job interviews.

The Importance of Emotional Quotient (EQ) in Job Interviews

When looking at this IQ list, one might be led to believe the person who has the highest IQ is the one who will get the job or is the most successful in life. Unless you are being interviewed by Goggle or some other company that invests twice as much as other companies in recruiting people based primarily on the highest IQ or higher education, many companies would rather consider a person's emotional quotient (EQ) and attitude over IQ and higher degrees in their hiring decisions. Today, many companies are incorporating EQ tests into their interviews and adopting EQ training into their business culture.

Most people are familiar with IQ, but few people are aware of their emotional intelligence (EI) or emotional quotient (EQ). In many cases, employers will hire a candidate whose EQ is higher than their IQ.

Your EQ score rates your ability or capacity to perceive, understand, control, evaluate and express emotions—yours and other people's emotions. How you deal with your emotions determines how well you work with and get along with other people, particularly people in your workplace.

People with high EQ scores are considered confident individuals with good communications and leadership skills that have good control over their emotions. This makes them better suited for group or team environments, such as in the workplace, than people with low EQ scores—characteristics that the IQ scores does not measure or reveal.

Besides controlling their emotions well, people with high EQ scores are highly motivated and productive; face change, variety and challenges head on because they do not fear failure; and show greater endurance and perseverance under long-term struggles and hardship than people with low EQ scores.

If the definition of a high EQ score sounds strangely familiar to the definition of an alpha type person, you would be right because many of the qualities of a person with a high EQ score parallel the qualities of alpha types.

Just as there are IQ tests you can take online, there are many EQ tests and assessments on the Internet you can take for free.

Here are some online EQ tests you can take:

- https://memorado.com/emotional_quotient

- http://www.ihhp.com/free-eq-quiz

- https://www.arealme.com/eq/en

- https://www.mindtools.com/pages/article/ei-quiz.htm

- http://personality-testing.info/tests/EI.php

- http://greatergood.berkeley.edu/ei_quiz

- http://www.iq-test.net/eq-test.html

As I mentioned, many scientists, psychologists, researchers and educators have been stating since the 1990s that your emotional intelligence (EI) or emotional quotient (EQ) is more important than your IQ in determining your overall intelligence and your success in the workplace and in life in general.

Allow me to introduce some of those experts to you.

Travis Bradberry knows all about EQ testing and training. Dr. Bradberry holds a Dual Ph.D. in Clinical and Industrial-Organizational Psychology from the California School of Professional Psychology. He is a world-renowned expert in emotional intelligence, the award-winning coauthor of the 2009 book *Emotional Intelligence 2.0* and cofounder of TalentSmart, the world leader in emotional intelligence tests and training.

TalentSmart provides EQ resources to over 75 percent of Fortune 500 companies; and the talentsmart.com website provides many case studies showing how EQ training and tests have helped many companies.

TalentSmart's own studies of people at all levels of work in different industries of every region of the world reveal that 90 percent of your top performers at work have high EQ scores; and that people with high EQ scores also make an average of $29,000 per year more than people with low EQ scores.

When TalentSmart tested factors that predict a person's greatest chance for success in the workplace, they included emotional intelligence in addition to 33 other necessary workplace skill sets in those tests. The results revealed that of all these skill sets, emotional intelligence provided the strongest predictor of performance success—58 percent—in all types of job markets.

Dr. Bradberry points out that your EQ level is not fixed at birth; it can be developed, reshaped, improved and increased to produce positive impacts in your life. He states that the whole person is made up of IQ, EQ and personality; each independent of each other; and that of the three, only EQ can be developed and altered. Dr. Bradberry argues that you need to increase your EQ level to increases your chances of success in your career as well as all other areas of your life.

Daniel Goleman holds a Ph.D. from Harvard and is the author of the international bestsellers *Emotional Intelligence*, *Working with Emotional Intelligence*, *Social Intelligence*, and the acclaimed business bestseller *Primal Leadership*.

In Dr. Goleman's 1996 New York Times #1 Best Seller book *Emotional Intelligence* that sold over 5 million copies worldwide in 40 languages, he suggested your emotional intelligence quotient (EQ) is more important than the traditional intelligence quotient (IQ) in determining your success in life. Dr. Goleman argues that the reason why people with high IQs can fail or flounder in life and people with modest IQs can be successful in life is because the successful person with the modest IQ has a higher emotional intelligence (EQ) than the unsuccessful person with the high IQ but lower EQ.

This argument by Dr. Goleman can also help explain the driving force behind that long list of successful and wealthy people making millions or even billions of dollars; people that are high school or college dropouts or without any college education at all. A ***high EQ*** that Dr. Goleman points out along with some ***true grit*** that Dr. Duckworth talks about and "The Duke" displayed is a winning combination for great success in life—and in your job interview.

Focusing on developing one's EQ is not just for people seeking to impress hiring managers in job interviewers or current employees seeking to perform better at their jobs. Higher EQ levels also produce better leaders. In his international bestseller, *Primal Leadership: Unleashing The Power of Emotional Intelligence*, Dr. Goleman, along with co-authors Drs. Richard Boyatzis and Annie McKee, performed research on workplaces led by over 3,870 executives. After their research, they discovered that the most effective business leaders are those who understand and harness their emotional intelligence in leading their people.

Like Dr. Bradberry and TalentSmart, Dr. Goleman and his colleagues teach that your emotional intelligence involves malleable traits that can be learned, taught, changed, developed and managed. Rather than focusing on one's IQ in predicting a person's success in life, Goleman suggests people develop their EQ in order to increase their chances for a more successful life.

Clearly, understanding and developing your emotional intelligence will help provide you greater success in your job interviews and career.

If you're convinced in your mind that neither IQ nor EQ levels can be altered to increase your chances of success in job interviews or in life in general, many scientific researchers and educators, such as Carol Dweck, would soundly disagree with you.

Dr. Carol Dweck is a world-renowned research psychologist, a Yale graduate who held professorships at Harvard and Columbia Universities; and is now the Lewis and Virginia Eaton Professor of Psychology at Stanford University. Over the past two decades, she has debunked the idea that intelligence, talents, skills and abilities are fixed, uncontrollable traits from birth that produce success in life. Instead, she advocates the theory that these traits can be developed and changed; and that hard work, learning, training, attitude, persistence and perseverance are what make people successful in life.

In her highly acclaimed book, *Mindset: The New Psychology of Success*, Dr. Dweck explains how people become biased in their thinking or "*mindset*" about their intelligence, skills, talents and abilities. She argues that people can have either a *fixed mindset* that believe they can't change their innate intelligence, skills, talents and abilities or they have a *growth mindset* that believe they can change and mold their malleable intelligence, skills, talents and abilities through hard work, learning, training and perseverance.

According to Dr. Dweck, having a **fixed mindset** places you at a disadvantage because you believe you can't improve yourself to become more successful in life. Since you think your traits are permanently fixed, that mindset reduces your motivation to try harder to improve and become more successful in life. People with fixed mindsets fear failure because failure to them is a reflection of their perception of a permanent level of intelligence, skills, talents and abilities.

Growth mindset individuals accept failure as part of the learning and growth process to make them better in life. Since these individuals believe failure is part of the process, they continue to persevere and develop themselves to become better in life despite any failures.

Your mindset will also affect your attitude about yourself, your life and your chances of success in a job interview.

Dr. Arthur Poropat of Griffith University's School of Applied Psychology in Australia, a university that is ranked in the top 200 by the QS World University Rankings in 2015, conducted the largest ever study of personality and academic performance based on five fundamental personality traits, also known as the Big Five personality traits or the Five-Factor Model (FFM) of personality—conscientiousness, openness, agreeableness, emotional stability and extraversion.

The results of his research, that included data from tens of thousands of students was published as an article, titled *Other-rated personality and academic performance: Evidence and implications*, in the August 2014 edition of the research journal *Learning and Individual Differences*, Volume 34 that can be viewed on sciencedirect.com.

Dr. Poropat's research concluded that these five factors of personality trump intelligence (IQ) and is more important than intelligence when it comes to success in learning and education. In fact, Dr. Poropat's study showed **conscientiousness** (being thorough, careful, efficient, organized and systematic) and **openness** (being open to experiences) is four times more important than IQ in predicting academic success.

- **Openness** to experience includes active imagination (fantasy); aesthetic sensitivity (toward beauty, appearance, arts and taste); preference for variety and change; intellectual curiosity (the desire to learn, explore, discover and experience new things); and being connected to one's inner feelings (an EQ quality).

- **Agreeableness** (another EQ quality) is being kind, considerate, sympathetic, warm and cooperative.

- **Emotional stability** (another EQ quality) is the ability to remain calm and even keel under pressure or when experiencing stress.

- **Extraversion** is an extrovert who is a highly sociable, talkative, energetic and assertive personality type that tends to be more outgoing and happy than your introvert type.

Dr. Poropat's research study shows that factors other than IQ can produce success not only in school but in the workplace and in life. As with Drs. Travis Bradberry, Daniel Goleman and Carol Dweck and their studies and theories about success, Dr. Poropat also stated that these five personality traits for academic success are malleable traits that can be changed and developed by each individual; and that hard work, effort and perseverance go a long way in predicting a person's success in learning and education.

Even Presidents Go Through the Job Interview Process

These arguments by so many scientists, psychologists, researchers and educators (the experts) explaining why people with high IQs but low EQs can fail or flounder in life, and people with modest IQs but high EQs can be successful in life was born out in our 2016 US presidential election between Hillary Clinton and Donald Trump.

Hillary Clinton went to Yale Law School, an Ivy League school, where she graduated with a Yale Juris Doctor degree. Secretary Clinton has a reported IQ of 140, three points above her husband, Bill Clinton, who has a reported IQ of 137. Together, Hillary and Bill Clinton represented the status quo of the elite, the Clinton political machine, and the political powerhouse in Washington. Everything seemed in Secretary Clinton's favor to win the US presidential election—based on her high IQ and political qualifications that is. As far as money goes, Clinton raised $1.3 billion as of October 19, 2016. Even the exit polls and pundits had Hillary Clinton winning in state after state over Donald Trump.

Donald Trump, on the other hand, graduated with a bachelor's degree in economics from the Wharton School of the University of Pennsylvania—an Ivy League business school. He was a businessman, an outsider to Washington with no political experience and no military background; a first for our nation whose presidents always had either one or both of these qualifications. Many would argue that Donald Trump was the most unqualified person to be our nation's next president. As far as money goes, Trump raised only $795 million as of October 19, 2016.

Despite the odds against Donald Trump, he handedly won the 2016 presidential election over Hillary Clinton. Both candidates went through the fiery trial of their job interview process in front of the American public throughout their campaigns; and yet their hiring manager (over 130 million American voters) selected Donald Trump over Hillary Clinton for the job as our nation's 45th president.

Why? . . . How?

Part of our nation and other nations are scratching their heads in disbelief, shell-shocked by this surprising political upset that many are calling America's "Brexit". The other half of our nation and other nations are celebrating in absolute amazement, joy and happiness. Journalists, pollsters and the rest of the media are spinning out of control at this stunning upset and historic win by Donald Trump. As "The Donald" (excuse me, as "The Mr. President") would say: ***This is HUGE!***

You could say like these "experts" I've quoted that Donald Trump had a higher EQ with perhaps a lower IQ than Hillary Clinton; while Hillary Clinton had a higher IQ with a much lower EQ than Donald Trump. Hillary Clinton had the higher **IQ** and **political experience and qualifications**—the *technical fit*, but Donald Trump had the *grit* and higher *EQ* that could connect with the American voters—the *cultural fit*.

That's why Donald Trump got the job from his new employer—the American people; and started his new job on Friday, January 20, 2017 as our nation's 45th president at his employer's office—the Oval Office—on 1600 Pennsylvania Avenue for a whopping $1. This is not a typo—I said *one dollar* because Trump did not want any salary to work for the American people; however, he is required by law to receive payment for his services to the US government.

*"**Back the presidential bus up just one minute!**" you exclaim. "Didn't Hillary Clinton win the popular vote over Donald Trump? How can you say Trump has a higher EQ that could connect with the American voters when Hillary had the higher popular vote?" you ask.*

It's because the **popular vote** in American politics is as misleading as the exit polls, pundits and biased media were about Clinton's "clear victory". True, Hillary is popular among the masses—she has a certain level of EQ (emotional quotient) that connects with American voters. However, her EQ was *not high enough*. In other words, she was *"not popular enough"* to move the voters she needed to come out and vote for her. She was not popular enough to muster the necessary votes to secure the magical 270 (out of a possible 538) **electoral votes** needed to win the presidency. She was not popular enough to convince a few thousand more voters to come out and vote for her in those swing states. Was she popular? Yes. Was she popular enough to win the election? No.

According to the US Elections Project, of the roughly 231,556,622 eligible voters in the 2016 presidential election, roughly over 134,765,650 (58.4%) actually voted. Among those who voted, the New York Times reported on November 21, 2016, the tallied votes that were still coming in showed Clinton's 48% of the popular vote was increasing over Trump's 47% of votes—that's definitely more votes than Trump as far as this "popularity contest" goes.

However, winning the election as the US President is not just about winning more votes; it's about winning more votes in battleground states (swing states that either candidate could win) that provide a larger number of winner-takes-all **electoral votes**. Although the statistics on the **popular vote** do not show it, Trump was *"more popular"* than Clinton in getting enough people to vote for him in those battleground states—the states which gave him the lead in **electoral votes**. Trump didn't use a higher IQ to win those extra votes; he used a higher EQ to win the hearts of those people in those states to get them to come out and vote for him.

When it came down to winning those key battleground states, Trump unexpectedly won those states that all the exit polls, pundits and biased media said Clinton would win. In other words, in those states, Donald Trump was *more popular* than Hillary Clinton—this is what got Trump the **270+ electoral votes** he needed to win the election. Even though Senator Clinton won the **popular vote**, it was Trump who was *more popular* in those swing states that got him the job as President of the United States of America. Was Trump popular? Yes. Was he popular enough to win the election? Yes.

Only a few thousand votes decided who our 45th president would be—**Donald Trump**. For instance, Trump won Wisconsin (a swing state with 10 electoral votes) with just 27,257 more votes than Clinton. Trump won Michigan (16 electoral votes) with only 10,704 more votes than Clinton. One could argue that if Hillary Clinton was popular enough to convince those few thousand more voters in swing states like Wisconsin and Michigan to come out and vote for her, we would have sworn in Hillary Clinton as our 45th president on January 20, 2017.

Translation: *Your vote counts.* Think about that next time you decide *not* to cast your vote, regardless of your political affiliation.

This marks the fourth time in US history that a candidate won the *popular vote* but lost the presidency to another candidate who won the *electoral vote*. Like Hillary Clinton, the three other candidates who won the popular vote but lost the electoral vote were all **Democrats** (Al Gore in 2000; Grover Cleveland in 1888; and Samuel Tilden in 1876). Like Donald Trump, the three other candidates who lost the popular vote but won the electoral vote—and became president—were all **Republicans** (George W. Bush in 2000; Benjamin Harrison in 1888; and Rutherford B. Hayes in 1876).

History does indeed repeat itself.

It's the same way in your job interview—it repeats itself. It probably won't be a higher IQ or higher degree that's going to get you the votes you need above your job-hunting competition to win that available position. It could come down to who has the higher EQ to win the hearts of those interviewers.

The ancient Greek storyteller Aesop's fable of the race between *The Tortoise and the Hare* is a parody of Clinton's premature election night *"victory"* celebration party on Election Day, the 8th of November, 2016 at the Jacob K. Javits Convention Center in New York. In attendance were start-studded celebrities, such as Katy Perry, Beyoncé, Jay Z, Jason Derulo, Lady Gaga, Melanie Griffith and Cher. The night was supposed to end with a fireworks display over the Hudson River capping off Secretary Clinton's *"speedy rabbit"* victory over the *"slow but steady tortoise"* Trump as our nation's 45th president. Instead, Clinton and her supporters went home in tears, hanging their heads in painful defeat.

As with many of life's events that reflect the fable of *The Tortoise and the Hare*; the moral of Hillary Clinton's presidential story will go down in history as: **Make sure the race is over before you *party like it's 1999.***

The Importance of Attitude in Your Job Interview

Attitude is all about how you carry yourself in the job interview. Your attitude, whether it's positive or negative, is affected by your thoughts, beliefs, emotions, feelings and opinions about someone or something.

A person with a positive, optimistic attitude sees themselves, their circumstances and their outlook on life through the lens of confident expectations of good, happiness and success regardless of the situation.

It's important for you to be in the right frame of mind during your job interview. I understand you could think of 50 other places you'd rather be than in a job interview, but during the interview is not the time to let those negative feelings about job interviews undermine the type of attitude you need to display in front of your interviewers.

Don't walk through that doorway into the interview room as if you are the character in the 14th century epic poem *Divine Comedy*, written by Dante Alighieri, who is walking through the vestibule of hell (Dante's Inferno) which bore the inscription over the doorway: *"Abandon all hope, ye who enter here."*

You're not that poor slob in *Divine Comedy* who, in our context about job interviews, allegorically has to make his journey through the chambers of hell filled with interviewers carrying pitch forks; past the purgatory of a barrage of questions; until you finally make your way to the paradise of a new job. You are not Dante in the *Divine Comedy* and your job interview is not a punishment; it is an opportunity for you to move forward to something better in your life.

You want your interviewers to see you as a person who has a positive attitude that they would enjoy working with; someone who is enthusiastic and excited about this job opportunity. Every workplace has its share of whiners, complainers and other types of people with negative, pessimistic attitudes that can pull people down at work. The last person your hiring manager and co-workers want to hire is another person with that type of attitude.

The workplace is going to challenge you with many problems you'll have to solve. Employers want to know if you are the type of person who can face these challenges with a positive attitude that believes he or she can solve problems and produce good results.

So give yourself permission to breathe, relax, smile, and think happy, confident, positive thoughts while you're in that job interview. Learn to loosen up and enjoy the interview experience. Don't be wound so tight that you can't think straight or laugh or respond correctly to humor.

One of my colleagues and I were newly hired network engineers for a large IT company. When he and I had a chance to talk about our interview experience, he told me that after his job interview he immediately went out and bought five new suits for work. Apparently, his interviewers told him tongue-in-cheek that everyone wears suits five days a week at work. They expected him to take that statement lightheartedly, but instead, he took them seriously and spent some hefty cash for five new suits. On his first day of work, when he was the only one wearing a suit and tie while everyone else was in their business casual slacks and jeans; that's when he realized that they were just having fun with him. That's what can happen to you when you are wound too tight during your job interview. So relax; your interviewers are people too. They like to smile and joke with you too during your interview.

As you move from junior to senior positions, your hiring manager and interviewers are going to expect you to display more confidence in yourself. Senior professionals are not only expected to show higher levels of knowledge and experience in a desired role, they are expected to show more leadership qualities which require confidence and a good attitude.

When you walk in that door to the interview room, walk in there with your head held high, your shoulders back and your chest out like you own the place; like you're the most important person in the world. Not with an arrogant air about you, but with a quiet confidence that says, "*I got this.*"

When you pick up that phone for your phone interview, sit or stand tall with your chest out and your shoulders back. You're in your office; not theirs. Breathe in slowly the fresh air of confidence that fills your lungs with strength, energy and power to perform well in that phone interview. You got this under control.

You are not at a disadvantage in the interview; you are on equal footing with your interviewers. After all, **they have just as big a need as you:** they need someone like you to fill a much needed position in their workplace; and you need someone like them to provide you a job.

Think of it like this: your interview with them is going to be either a win-win situation for both of you or lose-lose situation; not a win-lose situation. If they hire you, both of you win by fulfilling your needs: you filled their need for another professional and they fulfilled your need for a job. If they don't hire you, both sides lose in that situation: both you and the company have to continue interviewing; something both sides would rather end by you being the one they hire.

A positive attitude not only helps you have a more successful career; a positive outlook on life is better for your overall health. The well-known Mayo Clinic is one of the world's best hospitals and ranked number 1 on the list of nearly 5,000 "Best Hospitals" on the 2014–2015 U.S. News & World Report. The Mayo Clinic staff posted an article, titled *Positive thinking: Stop negative self-talk to reduce stress*, on their Mayoclinic.org website that suggests an optimistic or pessimistic attitude can affect your health and well-being.

The Mayo Clinic stated that the health benefits of positive thinking include, increased life span; lower rates of depression; lower levels of distress; greater resistance to the common cold; better psychological and physical well-being; reduced risk of death from cardiovascular disease; and better coping skills during hardships and times of stress.

Power Posture, Power Thoughts and Power Words for Job Interviews

Your attitude is also affected by your body posture, your thoughts and your own words while standing or sitting. Having the right posture— standing with your shoulders back and your chest out in a comfortable position or sitting upright or slightly forward in your chair—will not only make you feel more confident in yourself; your interviewers will notice your confidence and enthusiasm based on your posture too. It has long been proven that your posture affects your attitude and confidence just as your thoughts and words do.

How Posture Impacts Your Job Interview

In 2009, **Dr. Richard Petty**, Professor of Psychology at Ohio State University, and two other OSU alumni, Pablo Brinol and Benjamin Wagner, performed a research study of 71 students. In this study, students were asked to either sit upright with their shoulders back and their chest out or slouch in their chairs in front of a computer while they rated themselves as future professionals in a job. The results of the study, titled *Body posture effects on self-evaluation: A self-validation approach* was published in the February 2009 edition of the European Journal of Social Psychology.

This study found that students rated themselves more highly with confident, positive self-attitude for jobs when they sat upright than when they slouched in their chairs. In other words, when the students sat in a position of power—upright—they felt empowered; therefore, they rated themselves highly. When they slouched in their chairs—a position of weakness, they felt less empowered; therefore, they rated themselves low.

In 2012, **Dr. Amy Cuddy**, a social psychologist working as an Associate Professor of Business Administration at Harvard Business School and author of the multi-best seller book, *Presence: Bringing Your Boldest Self to Your Biggest Challenges*, gave a TED talk on TED.com, a nonprofit organization that shares ideas about technology, entertainment and design (TED) worldwide. Dr. Cuddy gave her talk, titled *Your body language shapes who you are*, at TEDGlobal 2012 in Edinburgh, Scotland which has been viewed more than 33 million times on TED.com.

Cuddy shared how her research and experiments along with colleagues Dana Carney and Andy Yap of UC-Berkeley show you can fake confident body postures of dominance and power, something she calls "**power posing**", for as little as two minutes, even when you don't feel confident, to increase testosterone levels in your body; decrease cortisol levels; and increase your desire for risk-taking which causes you to perform better in job interviews.

Dr. Cuddy's research states that power people and leaders—your alpha male types—show significantly higher levels of testosterone and significantly lower levels of cortisol than the less powerful beta male types.

Alpha types are people—male or female—who are more confident, extroverted, dominant, engaging, competitive, calm and non-reactive under pressure, assertive and charismatic than their beta counter-types. They also like standing out and speaking out in a crowd; and are risk takers because of their strong feelings of confidence and optimism, their desire to win in every situation, and their lack of fear in failing.

Beta types—male or female—are more careful and less optimistic about things which make them less confident, vocal, outgoing, confrontational, engaging and assertive than alpha types. They're more passive, timid, shy, quiet, introverted and reserved than their alpha counter-types.

Cortisol is a natural steroid hormone in your body, also referred to as a "stress hormone" that increases your adrenalin to prepare your body for "fight-or-flight" situations. When your cortisol levels increase, your body becomes flooded with glucose; your arteries become narrow and your heart rate increases; making you feel more nervous and excited and less at ease during job interviews.

Dr. Cuddy's research shows that if you posture your body in a way that reflects dominance, power and confidence—the byproduct of alpha types, your brain and mind will also think the same way, triggering your body and emotions to follow suit. This will help give you more confidence and put you at ease and in a stronger frame of mind during job interviews.

What Dr. Cuddy recommends job-hunting candidates do before meeting the interviewers at their job interview is to spend at least two minutes in private, such as in a bathroom, an elevator, a vacant room or at home before they leave, standing in a power position.

A standing power position is any alpha male standing position, such as standing with your shoulders back; your chest out; your head held looking straight ahead; your feet spread apart; and both hands resting confidently at your hips. Hold that position for at least two minutes to give your mind and body time to accept and adjust to that power position.

Dr. Cuddy is basically telling us to do with our bodies (power poses) what motivational speakers have been telling us for decades to do with our mind, thoughts, visualization and imagery techniques (power thoughts), and our words and vocalization (power words) to influence our self-talk in a positive way.

Dr. Cuddy's research on how power postures increase testosterone levels and decrease cortisol levels in your body may also lend a scientific explanation for why power thoughts and words taught by motivational speakers (such as Tony Robbins, Zig Ziglar and Jim Rohn) and by preachers of positive thinking (such as Norman Vincent Peale and Joel Osteen) actually work for so many people.

Whether we choose to listen to Dr. Cuddy or one of your favorite motivational speakers, mentors, life coaches or spiritual leaders; their end goal is the same: to help you become more confident, strong, positive, likeable and optimistic in your life, including in your job interviews.

How Power Thoughts and Power Words Impact Your Job Interview

Dr. Jim Taylor holds a Ph.D. in Psychology from the University of Colorado; is a former Associate Professor in the School of Psychology at Nova University in Ft. Lauderdale; and current adjunct professor at the University of San Francisco and the Wright Institute in Berkeley. He's worked with professional and Olympic athletes in football, baseball, triathlon, golf, cycling, tennis, skiing and other sports. He's been a consultant to the US and Japanese Ski Teams, the US Tennis Association, USA Triathlon; and was invited by Olympic committees of the US, Spain, France and Poland to speak to their athletes and coaches.

In a 2012 *Psychology Today* article, titled *Sport Imagery: Athletes' Most Power Mental Tool*, Dr. Taylor wrote, *"Imagery also isn't just a mental experience that occurs in your head, but rather impacts you in every way: psychologically, emotionally, physically, technically, and tactically. Think of mental imagery as weight lifting for the mind."*

Most of your top athletes and professional sports athletes use imagery techniques, also known as visualization, to rehearse their sport in their mind to maximize their sports performance. For example, football players will use sport imagery to visualize themselves catching the ball and running it in for a touchdown in the Super Bowl; baseball players visualize themselves hitting a homerun in the World Series; basketball players imagine themselves hitting 3-point shots in the NBA Finals; soccer (football) players see themselves kicking the game winning goal during the FIFA World Cup; and Olympians like Michael Phelps see themselves winning another gold medal while beating the living crap out of his South African rival swimmer, Chad Le Clos at the Rio Olympics. (I meant beating him in swimming. Don't send me any angry Phelps memes or *Angry Birds* my way for that remark.) These athletes are taught these imagery techniques to increase their positive self-talk and help them perform at higher levels when they are in competition.

After the Denver Broncos won the 2016 Super Bowl 50 Championship against the Carolina Panthers, Von Miller, the Super Bowl MVP, was surrounded by "Primetime" Deion Sanders and other NFL Network reporters. One of the reporters asked Miller if he ever saw himself where he's at now—at the Super Bowl level as the MVP. Von responded by saying, *"I do a lot of self-visualization and imagery . . . it was easy to say we're going to win the Super Bowl."*

Have you ever noticed how every time when the media asks a professional athlete how they feel about their upcoming championship game, they always respond the same way: *"It's just another game."*? In other words, these athletes are saying this all-important championship game is *no big deal.*

Their response is a visualization technique they've learned in order to make a very big event appear very small in their mind in order to control their emotions; stay focused and mentally tough; reduce their anxiety; and see their own selves as bigger than the championship game. They've trained themselves to make something very big look very small in their mind's eyes. Although they will prepare, train and practice as if it's the biggest event in their life; they train their minds with imagery and positive self-talk to think this game is just like any other regular season game.

You need to do the same thing for your job interviews. You should prepare as if each job interview is the biggest event in your life but you need make this important event appear very small in your mind to control your emotions; reduce your anxiety to help you relax; and make yourself feel bigger and more powerful than this interview.

The reason you become nervous, fearful and anxious about job interviews, speaking in public or other similar life events are because of your **negative** imagery, visualization and self-talk about the situation.

Instead you need to train yourself to think and see yourself in a **positive** light in these situations. Visualize and imagine yourself knocking that job interview out of the park. Imagine yourself being comfortable and confident in your interview. Visualize yourself giving a great introduction and answering your technical questions with great answers in your interview. See yourself feeling and speaking confident in your interview as you answer cultural fit questions. These visualization and imagery techniques will reinforce your positive self-talk and help give you the confidence and power to perform well in the actual job interview.

Power Postures, Thoughts and Words—Use It or Lose It

With this entire overwhelming evidence showing the advantages and benefits of power postures, power thoughts and power words, why not make use of all of the advice given by these experts?

The best part about these power poses, power thoughts and power words is that they are *free* just like the air you breathe; just take it in. I recommend you try using power thoughts and words from whichever motivational speaker or spiritual leader you choose along with Dr. Cuddy's 2-minute power pose, preferably in front of a full-length mirror if you have one available.

However, I recommend avoiding walking over hot coals prior to a job interview—sorry Tony Robbins; I couldn't resist. You might have heard or read the 2016 news report about Tony Robbins' four-day seminar, called *Unleash the Power Within*, where hot coals were spread outside the Kay Bailey Hutchinson Convention Center in Dallas, Texas where he was speaking. According to reports, more than 30 people were treated for burns and five people were taken to the hospital after the motivational speaker encouraged them to walk on hot coals as a way of conquering their fears; something Robbins regularly encourages his audiences to do at some of his seminars.

Perhaps they should have read the old proverb that asks the question: *"Can one walk on hot coals, and his feet not be seared?"* Proverbs 6:28 NKJV

You don't need to walk on hot coals to conquer your fears right before interviewing for a job, but you might need more than just a single 2-minute confidence boost right before your phone interview or in-person interview. So try these power poses, thoughts and words (including the ones from Tony Robbins if you prefer) several times hours or days before your interview. Give yourself a healthy dose of these confidence boosting techniques before and during your job interviews.

As Dr. Cuddy said at the close of her TED talk, *"Don't fake it 'til you make it. Fake it 'til you become it."* Keep faking those power postures, power thoughts and power words until they make sense to your mind, emotions and body.

Other Factors That Impact Your Job Interview

How the Chair You're Seated On Impacts Your Job Interview

The chair you're sitting on can also affect your posture in both phone interviews and in-person job interviews. I already shared with you Dr. Richard Petty's experiment with students that revealed the way you sit in a chair can affect the way you feel about yourself. If you sit in a position of power—upright—you will feel more empowered and confident in your job interview. If you slouch in your chair—a position of weakness, you will feel less empowered and confident in your job interview.

When taking your seat in the interview room, check the height of the chair to ensure it's at a comfortable height that allows you to sit upright. Go ahead and adjust the chair if you need to raise or lower it.

Oftentimes, interviewers will seat you on one of those swivel office chairs that allow you to adjust the height. The height adjuster is a metal lever underneath the right or left side of the seat. The chair lowers with your bodyweight when you pull up on the lever. To raise the seat, reach underneath the chair and pull the lever up with your fingers while rising up with your legs from your seat. The seat of the chair should rise on its own with you.

Some office swivel chairs will lean back when you sit in them. If your chair leans back, try to lock it in the upright position. If there is a lever underneath the chair to adjust the height, there should also be another lever underneath the chair that allows you to lock the chair in an upright position.

How Eye Contact and Head Level Impacts Your Job Interview

Two other areas that impact your job interview are your eye contact and head level.

Always maintain good eye contact when speaking with someone in the interview room. Maintaining eye contact shows you are not only a confident person but also someone interested in what the interviewers have to say. When you don't maintain good eye contact while having a conversation with someone, it makes you appear unsociable, weak and as if you have something to hide.

The type of person you want to project during your interview is a sociable, personable, confident person who is interested in the interviewer's questions and comments, and who is enthusiastic about working on their team. Good eye contact communicates those things to interviewers.

Obviously, your head should move naturally along with your eyes in the direction of the interviewer you are speaking with. Although you want to maintain a power posture when seated, you don't want to become stiff to the point that your eyes move but your head doesn't like a ventriloquist's dummy. Try to relax and allow your body movements to flow naturally with the person you are addressing in the room.

Although your head should be allowed to move freely from side-to-side as you look around the room at your interviewers, your head position should not be looking up toward the ceiling or down toward your hands, your watch, the table or the floor. Looking up makes you look like you're lost in space or at a loss for words. Looking down makes you look weak, a failure or loser, or as if you are lying. Looking down at your watch makes you look disinterested in being in the interview and that you have somewhere else to go. I'm sure the interviewers will oblige you if you give them that impression.

If the interviewer asks you a question you don't know the answer to, don't start looking around the room in desperation, waiting for some epiphany to reveal the answer to you. Just look the interviewer in the eyes and say, *"I don't know the answer to that question."* Your

174

straightforwardness and honesty makes you look much better in the eyes of the interviewer than that "deer in the headlights" look as you ponder the universe for the answer.

Where to Put Your Hands in Your Job Interview

Lastly, your hands and forearms should rest naturally on the desk in front of you. You can use your hands when you talk to emphasize a point, but don't wave your hands around constantly when you talk like a conductor of a symphony or something.

Never put your hands in your pockets while you are standing; don't hide your hands on your lap below the table in front of you; and don't put your hands in your pockets when seated during your interview. Sorry if I sound like your mother taking you to your first day at school when you were 5 years old. And don't forget to flush and wash your hands (just kidding; now I'm acting like your mother when you were 5).

There may be occasions in an interview where it would be acceptable to have your hand resting on your lap. For example, one job opportunity I interviewed for took place in the hiring manager's small office. I sat on a swivel office chair in front of the manager's desk. The front side of the manager's desk was paneled so I could not place my legs under the desk. There were also four other interviewers in the room to my left sitting in chairs against the wall.

In this scenario, I chose to keep my chair stationary up against the manager's desk facing the four interviewers. I placed my right arm and hand on top of the front end of the manager's desk, and my left hand rested comfortably on my left lap. My chair leaned back and it did not have an adjustment lever under the chair; however, I resisted the temptation to sit back in that chair. Instead, I sat upright in my chair the whole time.

I only had to turn my head to the right when talking with the hiring manager, and looked forward when talking with the four other interviewers who asked most of the questions. I was hired for this job interview that paid a six-figure salary that I had negotiated earlier with my staffing agency recruiter.

For another job interview I attended, my interviewers wanted me to meet them at a local restaurant during happy hour. There were four of us that sat on bar stools around a small tall table with just enough room for finger food and beverages which the hiring manager ordered for all of us to enjoy while I was being interviewed by them. Except for the fact that I was wearing a suit and tie while they and everyone else at their tables around us were wearing their normal business casuals, this was the ultimate relaxing interview environment.

It was obvious my interviewers wanted to see how I would fare in a relaxed outing with them—my cultural fit. However, this was still an interview, so I maintained good posture sitting upright as best as I could on my bar stool and maintained eye contact when speaking with them. When they asked me a question, I looked them in the eye and did not look down or up when I answered their interview questions. We laughed and joked as well; and overall had an enjoyable time together during the interview as we snacked on finger food and drank beverages. The best part was I got hired for that job too.

When you weigh all the mental (technical fit) and social (cultural fit) factors that go into successfully completing a job interview; the truth is you need IQ, EQ and attitude in your job interview. However, don't assume hiring managers and interviewers are going to weigh IQ above EQ and attitude. You need to show your interviewers you have the ability or capacity to learn, understand and apply information and skills by answering their technical questions satisfactorily—this is part of your IQ which translates to your technical fit. You also need to demonstrate to your interviewers that you have the ability or capacity to work well with other people, particularly people in your workplace and on your team, by your communications skills, personality, mannerisms and behavior—this is your EQ and attitude which translates to your cultural fit.

Job Interview Questions and Answers

The Interviewers that Ask the Questions

After all the introductions are out of the way, the interviewers will begin asking you technical questions. Most job interviews consist of 3–5 people on the phone or in the interview room with you as they ask you questions. Usually, all the people involved in the interview with you will take their turn asking you questions. Typically, the fewer interviewers there are, the more questions each interviewer will ask you. The more interviewers there are the fewer questions each will ask in order to stay within their scheduled interview timeframe. It is also normal for an interviewer who finished asking you questions to ask you a few more questions later on in the interview.

The hiring manager may or may not ask you technical questions depending on the manager's technical knowledge and experience. I've been in an interview with only two people—the hiring manager and the team lead. Both the hiring manager and the lead engineer asked me technical questions in that job interview.

It is also possible that some of the interviewers present on the phone or in the interview room won't ask you any questions. That may be the case when the interviewers have different skill sets, experience and qualifications, but they are all on the same team. Take my career field in IT for example. If I am being interviewed for a particular area, such as network engineering, then I may have only the network engineers on the phone or in the interview room ask me questions. However, if my resume shows I have both network engineering and security engineering experience, then both the network and security engineers may be brought in to interview me in both network and security engineering technologies. I've also been in a rare interview where there were six people in the room but only one person asked me technical questions because that person was the only one who had my type of network experience. The other people in the room had a system administrator experience but were on the same team with the network engineer questioning me.

Although the topics you see in the job description are the areas where the interviewers will focus their questions on; technologies outside the scope of the job description are also open game for questions if those technologies or certifications are listed in your resume.

How to Answer Questions in Your Job Interview

Don't be long-winded when giving your answers to the interviewer's questions. Keep your answers short and concise. Most questions can be answered in 30 seconds or less. With the exception of very few technical questions and your introduction where you would take more time to talk about yourself; if you are going over 30 seconds when answering a question, chances are you are using too many words to answer the question or you are struggling to answer the question.

If you don't know the answer, maintain eye contact with the person asking the question, be direct and tell the person you don't know the answer to that question. If you know part of the answer, go ahead and share what you do know so that the interviewer will at least give you partial credit for knowing portions of the subject. That may be more than what other candidates can answer about that particular question.

Sometimes an interviewer will ask you a question that doesn't make sense to you. It's not that you don't know the answer; you just didn't understand the question. If you don't understand an interviewer's question, let the interviewer know you're not sure what they're asking you. The interviewer asking the question or another interviewer will try to rephrase the question without giving away the answer.

You should demonstrate good communications skills throughout the entire interview process. The way you communicate with each interviewer will give them a sampling of your soft skills, your emotional quotient and your cultural fit with both their team and the company. Your communications skills in the interview reflect how you will communicate with everyone at work once you are hired.

Part of good communications is showing your interviewers you are a good listener. When someone else is talking, don't interrupt them for any reason. Wait until the person is done talking before you inject a comment, answer or question into the conversation. Don't dominate the conversation. Let your interviewers set the pace and focus of the conversation throughout the interview.

Never speak negatively about any past jobs, managers, supervisors, leadership, co-workers or company policies in the interview. Speaking negatively about past workplaces, assignments and people does not reflect negatively on them; it reflects negatively on *you*. It shows you lack the maturity and professionalism to keep those negative comments to yourself.

When asked why you left your last job, don't speak negatively about previous co-workers or managers. Even if those people or companies were the reasons you left those jobs. Try to put a positive spin on why you left those former companies. Show your interviewers that you have the maturity and class to speak well of former employers and colleagues. Talk more in terms of looking for new opportunities, challenges or other ways to increase your knowledge and experience in your field as reasons for deciding to move on from those companies.

These interviewers know that one day you'll leave their company too. If you start griping about former workplaces or colleagues, your interviewers know it will be only a matter of time that you will be griping about them in the future too. No one wants to hire someone like that.

Sometimes interviewers will bait you to see if you'll say negative things about your previous boss, colleagues or employer by asking you soft skill questions, such as *"Tell me about a difficult boss you had in the past and how you dealt with that"* or *"Tell me about a time you had to work with a difficult person on your team."* Don't take the bait and start throwing people under the bus and running over them forwards and backwards as if they were creatures from a zombie apocalypse. That's not what your interviewer wanted to hear from you. Maintain your composure and share how you handled those conflicts in the workplace with confidence, maturity and professionalism.

How to Answer Questions about Salary in Your Job Interview

On rare occasions, one of the interviewers might ask you what is your desired compensation or salary expectation. It is taboo for you to bring up your salary or benefits during your interview. Doing so implies you are more interested in the money and benefits than the job; this will most certainly reflect poorly on you in front of your interviewers.

But what do you do when one of the interviewers, such as the hiring manager, brings up the topic of salary?

Do you start negotiating your salary right there on the spot? Do you go over with the interviewers what hourly rate or annual salary you already agreed to with your staffing agency recruiter? The answer to all of these questions is typically **no**. You should not discuss your desired salary or benefits with the interviewers regardless if you previously agreed to a salary with your recruiter. Do not reveal your specific hourly rate or annual salary to the interviewers that you negotiated with a staffing agency recruiter. This rule also applies if you are being interviewed over the phone.

First, let's take the case where you've already agreed to an hourly rate or annual salary with the recruiter.

Once you established your desired compensation with the staffing agency recruiter, the recruiter sent your salary request along with your resume to the employer. The fact that you're sitting in that interview room means the employer—more specifically, the hiring manager and that company's human resources department—has agreed to pay your desired salary. The hiring manager would not have asked to interview you if their company could not afford you.

Interviewers that ask you about your compensation under these conditions are either inexperienced at best or unprofessional at worst. If the hiring manager wants to talk with you about your salary requirements, the manager should do so in private; not with all the other interviewers listening in on that conversation. The interviewer who asks you about your desired salary in front of the other interviewers either doesn't know they're not supposed to ask that question about money in front of everyone or they don't care that you've already arranged your compensation through your recruiter. In either case, you should avoid discussing your desired salary with them.

The only person in the interview room who has the right to ask you about your desired compensation is the hiring manager because he or she is the one who will approve your salary in coordination with the HR department. The hiring manager knows what each person is making for their position on his team you will be joining if you are hired (because he approved their salaries); and some of those team members are on that phone or in that interview room with you. However, the rest of the interviewers present do not have the right to know what your desired compensation is *before* or *after* you are hired.

If it is someone other than the hiring manager asking you about your salary during your job interview, they are being nosy and out of line. They just want to know if you will be making more or less money than them when you are hired. If the hiring manager or team lead presiding over the interview is professional and on top of things, he or she will intervene and not permit an interviewer to ask you any salary questions.

Those other interviewers should not know what each other's salaries are; nor should they be permitted to know what you will make if you get hired. Many problems can occur when company employees or contractors talk about their salaries amongst themselves: someone is going to come out on the short end of that conversation and realize they are getting paid less for doing the same job as the other person.

The hiring manager should know better not to ask you your desired salary in front of the other interviewers because some of those people sitting across from you in the interview room will become your co-workers if you are hired. When you start working with them, they'll already know what you make because you shared your salary information with them in your interview.

Bad things can come out of sharing your salary information with job interviewers because interviewers have egos too. If you quote an hourly rate or annual salary that is more than what these interviewers negotiated for themselves, one or several of them might vote against hiring you because you—a newbie—would be making more money than they who have been working there longer than you. They'll try to get the hiring manager to hire someone who will be making less money than them. This will make it more difficult for the hiring manager to hire you even if he or she thinks you're the best person for the job.

Equally worse is these interviewers might not welcome you with open arms on their team, nor be as helpful as they might have been once you're hired because they know you are making more money than them. Sounds pretty unprofessional and you're right, it is but that's the reality of interviews conducted by company employees and contractors.

Then what should you do when asked about salary in the interview?

You have to be tactful in deflecting the question. By *deflecting* I mean you need to simply move or direct the conversation about money from that interview room to your staffing agency. Kindly and respectfully tell the interviewer that you've already agreed to a salary with your staffing agency, so there is no need to go over your salary. This should send a signal to the interviewers that you do not want to discuss salary; and all the interviewers should get the message, back off the salary question and move on to the next topic.

If they don't get the message the first time, you can reword the deflection again by telling them you're satisfied with what your staffing agency or recruiter is offering you for the position; and should they (the hiring manager and HR) offer you the job; you are ready to start working for them.

I've had interviewers ask me about my salary expectations, and I answered them the way I'm suggesting you answer them. It works for me every time.

However, if the interviewer continues to press you for an answer about your desired compensation, you should tell the interviewer that your recruiter would be happy to discuss your salary requirements with them; but you would rather not talk money or benefits in the interview because you're there to talk about the job. The good news is you already know they can afford you—that's the beauty of working through a staffing agency.

Don't be upset when interviewers ask you about your salary. It's a sign the interviewers are interested in hiring you and sometimes they just want to know if they can afford you.

Let's consider another scenario where you didn't get the job interview through a staffing agency.

Suppose you got the interview as a result of submitting your resume on the company's online career website; and during the interview, one of the interviewers pops the question about salary. You can't deflect the question to a staffing agency recruiter because you didn't go through one.

True, but you should still deflect the question for two reasons:

1. You don't want all the interviewers to know your salary.

2. You have greater leverage to negotiate a higher salary after they decide to hire you.

You don't want all the interviewers to know your salary.

First, interviews rarely involve only one interviewer. Jobs where you may experience a one-on-one interview between you and the hiring manager only may occur in businesses such as retail or restaurants. For other types of companies, there may be between 3 to 6 people interviewing you in-person or over the phone for that open position.

With this many people in the interview, there's usually several interviewers in that room who should not be privy to salary information of other workers in their company. The hiring manager or team lead in that interview should understand this just as in the previous situation where you have a recruiter representing you.

By sharing your salary requirements in this situation, you again run the risk of facing the same challenges that come with revealing your salary with your future co-workers.

You have greater leverage to negotiate a higher salary after they decide to hire you.

Secondly, you have greater leverage in negotiating your salary if you wait until after the company has decided to hire you than you would if you tried to negotiate your salary during your job interview. Once the company's HR department sends you an offer letter, you now have a greater advantage to negotiate a better salary than you did when you were in the interview. Why? Because the offer letter means the hiring manager and the rest of the interview team want you above all the other job-seeking candidates they've interviewed. This gives you some leverage now in your response to the HR department concerning your salary.

If the salary in the offer letter is too low, you can reply with a counter-offer asking for more money. Yes, this is taking a risk. HR can either agree to match your counter-offer or refuse your counter-offer and choose not to hire you. That's the beauty of being a free agent—you control the risk and reward. If your counter-offer is not an outrageous amount above the original offer, the HR department is going to be more willing to pay you the higher amount because you've already gone through the vetting process and have the seal of approval from the hiring manager and the other interviewers that you are the right person for the job.

You are taking a greater risk by asking for that higher salary during the interview process—before their decision to hire you—than you are asking for that higher salary after the decision to hire you. If you try to ask for more money while the hiring manager is still interviewing other candidates for the job, the hiring manager may be more inclined to pick the candidate with a lower salary than you for the job.

The key is to try and deflect and postpone revealing your desired compensation until after the decision to hire you. You do not want to find yourself haggling over your salary with the people who are interviewing you—the people deciding whether or not to hire you. You want to reserve your salary negotiations for the HR department with whom you can be a little more hardheaded without offending your interviewers and negatively impacting their decision to hire you. Once they've decided to hire you, then you can talk money with greater assertiveness and leverage.

So let the employer's HR department make the first move in making you an offer. You might even be pleasantly surprised to find the employer's offer is equal to or higher than the amount you planned to ask for the job.

So how do you deflect their salary question in this situation?

You should use the same strategy as when you are represented by a recruiter: *deflect* the question by moving or directing the conversation about money from that job interview to another time and place. In other words, kindly and respectfully tell the interviewers that you would enjoy working with them, but you prefer to not talk about money until they've made a decision to hire you. Again, this should send a signal to the interviewers, especially to the hiring manager, that you do not want to discuss salary, and all the interviewers should get the message and move on to the next topic.

You could also throw in phrases such as, *"I'm willing to stay within the budget projected for this position"* or *"I'll accept any reasonable offer."* This should satisfy their curiosity as to whether or not they could afford you and, hopefully, not press you any further about your salary requirements.

Telling the interviewers that you are willing to stay within budget does not mean you can't negotiate your salary with the HR department after the hiring manager selected you for the job. It just means you are willing to work things out with HR; and if the salary is too low for you, you can either give HR your counter-offer or walk away as a last strategy to get what you want.

If your resources allow you the opportunity to walk away from a low salary offer, let HR know that you mean business about your desired salary and will pass on this job opportunity if you are not paid what you want. HR already knows the hiring manager and his or her team members want you on their team, so they're going to think twice about denying your counter-offer. I've done this several times in the past and it has worked in my favor.

After one job interview, the hiring manager wanted to hire me. I was using a staffing agency recruiter who told me the salary that the employer wanted to pay me. I wanted more, so I gave my counter-offer to the recruiter to pass on to the employer. I specifically told the recruiter to tell the employer that if they did not want to pay me my desired salary, I did not want the job. This was a gutsy move but I was willing to take the risk in order to reap the reward. If the employer decided to pass on me, I had enough resources to continue my job search elsewhere.

I didn't hear from the recruiter for a week and thought the hiring manager decided to pass on my counter-offer. However, at the end of that week, the recruiter contacted me and told me the employer agreed to pay me my desired compensation; and I started working for that employer. The beautiful thing of it was that none of the other colleagues in my office knew how much money I was making for that job because I never talked salary with my interviewers who had now become my colleagues at work.

Lastly on this subject of being asked salary questions, if your personality does not hold up well under the pressure of the hiring manager or another interviewer asking you to talk about salary; and you feel compelled to discuss your salary; then do yourself a favor and start with a salary range instead of a specific salary number. This way you give yourself a better chance of falling within the company's budgeted salary for that position. If you quote a specific salary number that is above what they are offering for the position, you stand the chance of losing out on the job altogether because the hiring manager knows they can't afford what you want or they can hire someone for a lot less.

How to Answer Questions about How Soon Can You Start Working

Oftentimes, at the end of a phone or in-person interview, I'm asked the question: "*How soon can you start?*" Obviously, this is a good sign when you are asked this question because it means your interviewers are interested in hiring you. As tempting as it might be to belch out, "*Right now!*" don't do it. That answer makes you sound desperate; not excited or enthusiastic for the job.

If you are currently employed, tell your interviewers that you need at least two weeks to give your current employer notice of your resignation. This will let your interviewers know you are a person of integrity, respect, responsibility and fairness by doing the right thing in giving your current employer a two-week notice. The hiring manager and interviewers know you will afford them the same courtesy when the time comes for you to leave their company too. This scores huge points in the emotional quotient (EQ) department in the eyes of your interviewers.

If you are currently unemployed, show your interviewers you want the job but also understand there is a process involved by saying, "*I'll need some time to get in-processed and on-boarded with my staffing agency* (if you're working through a staffing agency), *but as soon as that process is done, I'll be free to start.*"

If you need some time to take care of a few personal things before starting work, go ahead and tell your interviewers you can start in a week or two weeks. If you need some extra weeks to move and relocate to your new employer's location, let the hiring manager know of your plans to relocate and the need for extra time for the move.

In one interview, the hiring manager knew I was in the same state as their company but would possibly have to relocate if he hired me because of the distance between my home and the job site. Therefore, he asked me what my plan was concerning my commute to work if I were hired. I told him I planned to move to their location. After the interview, they hired me for the job; at which time I asked for three weeks to move to their location and get settled in which they granted me.

Questions to Ask the Interviewers and Closure

More often than not, the hiring manager or another person leading the interview is going to ask you, *"**Do you have any questions for us?**"* at the conclusion of your interview. Don't take lightly the interviewer's invitation to you to ask them questions. You would be doing yourself a disservice if you pass on asking them any questions. Doing so shows your lack of preparation; lack of interest in the company; and will cause you to miss out on another opportunity to shine one last time above the other candidates interviewing for this job.

The entire interview process is about you making yourself stand out above all the other job-hunting candidates they plan to interview; and this last part of your interview should be used for that same goal. You should be ready to ask good, engaging *open-ended* questions that will require your interviewers to provide you more than just a yes or no answer.

Hopefully, you did your homework and researched the company; you read through the previous *Before the Interview* chapter on the do's and don'ts when asking interviewers your questions; and you prepared 2–3 questions ahead of time. You can write or type out these questions and have them in front of you for a phone interview or bring them with you to the in-person interview so that you remember to ask them at the end. I usually type these questions on my computer; print it out on one 8 by 11 inch sheet of paper; and then cut the sheet down to size to fit in my small portfolio I normally bring with me to interviews.

Closing Statements at the End of Your Job Interview

After the interviewers have answered your last question, don't wait for them to ask you if you have any closing statements because they might not ask you if you have any last words. Take the initiative to give them your closing statements immediately after they've answered your last question.

In your final closing statements, there are two things you need to do:

1. Thank the interviewers.

2. Ask for the in-person interview (for phone interviews) or for the job (for in-person interviews).

Thank the Interviewers for Inviting You to the Job Interview

First, you should always thank the interviewers for taking time out of their busy schedules to interview you. This lets the interviewers know you get it; you understand that they have work to do but they're on this phone or in that room with you to make this all about *you*—this is your interview, not theirs.

Ask the Interviewers for the Job

Secondly, ask for the job if this is an in-person interview. If it's a phone interview, ask for the opportunity to interview with them in person. The greatest salesperson in the world will not make a single sale until they ask for the sale. The answer is always no until you ask for the sale. If you don't ask, you can't have. After everything the hiring manager has told you about the company; after all the questions you were asked; let the interviewers know you are still interested in the open position and you are still enthusiastic about working with them.

You could combine both the thank you and asking for the in-person interview or the job in a couple of closing sentences. You could say something simple such as the following:

For the phone interview:

I'd like to take this time to say thank you to all of you for taking time out of your busy day to interview me. I'm very interested in this job, and I would enjoy taking the next step with an in-person interview with all of you.

For the in-person interview:

I'd like to take this time to say thank you to all of you for taking time out of your busy day to interview me. I'm very interested in this job, and I would enjoy working with all of you on your team.

By simply letting the interviewers know you're interested in the job and would enjoy working with them is telling them you want the job. That's all they need to hear from you to reassure them you still want the job after being grilled by them with so many questions. They may not tell you on the spot that you'll be invited back for an in-person interview or you've got the job, but you will have made a clear impression on their minds that you want the job.

Don't say, "***I want this job***", because those words make you appear desperate and it sounds like you just want the job and don't care about working with them.

Don't ask, "***When can I start?***", because that makes you come across as arrogant and as if you blindly presume you've already beat out all the competition before all the competition has had a chance to interview.

Can you take a more aggressive or assertive approach in asking your interviewers for the job?

Certainly, but I recommend doing so only if you sense that the interviewers like you for either your **technical fit** or **cultural fit** or both.

I went through a particularly grueling in-person job interview for a senior network engineer position where I was asked question after question by six interviewers who were also senior network engineers. They asked me a lot of questions that I didn't have the answers to. I was certain I was not the best technically fit engineer for that position but I was still very interested in the job and I wanted to work there.

Although I wasn't the smartest pea in the pod of candidates they would interview for this job, I could sense the interviewers enjoyed talking with me, and I felt I connected with them too. In other words, I knew I nailed it when it came to my emotional quotient (EQ) and cultural fit for the job.

So in my closing statements, I asked for the job more aggressively by putting on a big smile and telling the interviewers that I was very interested in the job and would love to work with each of them. Then I added with a smile, "*So what can I do to convince you guys to hire me?*"

The hiring manager responded, "*Give me a big sack of cash.*" (That tells you how poorly I performed with my technical answers in the interview.)

However, since I showed them my enthusiasm in wanting to work with them; and because we connected in common interests during our discussion that showed my cultural fitness; they hired me for the job that paid a six-figure salary that I previously negotiated with my staffing agency recruiter.

That's the power of asking for the job.

CHAPTER FOUR

After the Interview—Now What?

When you reach the end of your rope, tie a knot in it and hang on.
Franklin D. Roosevelt

Congratulations!

You did it! You made it through your interview—Congratulations!

In the closing scene of the 2003 animated movie *Finding Nemo* produced by Pixar, all the fish in the dentist's aquarium finally made their long-awaited escape after many failed attempts to break free from their watery prison in that dentist's office. They successfully turned their fish tank into a place that only Pigpen could love in a Charlie Brown special.

When the dentist placed all of the fish in separate plastic bags to clean the tank, each fish secretly rolled themselves to freedom out the open window like *American Ninja Warrior* contestants or *Spartan Race* competitors. They tumbled across the dangerous obstacles of a busy city street and hurled themselves over the water bank the way Olympic runners would throw themselves across the finishing line into the ocean's winning circle. As they bobbed together on the ocean's welcoming surface within their little plastic bags of freedom rejoicing over their victory; silence settles in among them.

Then one fish asks the all-important question: *"Now what?"*

That's sort of the way you feel after you completed your job interview. After jumping through so many hoops and making your way over so many obstacles to get to that all-important interview; you did it and it's over. Now you're finally sitting there in silence, free again to contemplate what just took place. You made it out of the confines of that interview room alive. You breathe a great sigh of relief like someone who was just let out of jail (or *Dante's Inferno*).

Like so many professional sports athletes waiting to find out if they made the team or if they're going to be cut, you're on the bubble waiting for what the future holds for you after completing your job interview.

You feel good about where you are now but you're still in this bubble, like those fish, asking yourself, "***Now what?***"

Here are a few things to consider while you wait out your time after a job interview:

- Sending thank you notes

- Perfecting your craft

- Other job opportunities

- The wait and the response

Sending Thank You Notes

Sending a thank you note to the hiring manager immediately after the interview thanking the manager for giving you the opportunity to interview for the job is still relevant advice today. It shows the hiring manager you do business in a professional and courteous manner. Using the thank you note is also a great opportunity to ask for the in-person interview (for phone interviews) or job (for in-person interviews) again, as you did toward the end of your interview, by letting the hiring manager know that you are excited about the opportunity to join his or her team.

If you plan to send the hiring manager a thank you note, try to send the note within 24 hours of completing your job interview. With today's technology, your thank you note can easily be sent via email to the hiring manager if you have access to their email address. Snail mail should be avoided due to postal delays that can occur internally and externally to the hiring manager's company.

With advances in technology and services come changes in the way people do business. This is also true with the thank you note after a job interview. When you are working through a staffing agency, chances are you may not have access to the email address or phone number of the hiring manager. Why? Because the middle man—the staffing agency—is there to be a buffer between the employer and you.

Many hiring managers prefer to communicate with candidates through the staffing agency; not directly with candidates. This gives the hiring manager the distance they oftentimes prefer to have between themselves and multiple job-hunting candidates interviewing for the job.

You can attempt to get the hiring manager's email address from your staffing agent, but don't be surprised if you are told the hiring manager prefers not to provide you their email or phone number before or after your interview. Typically, what ends up happening is the staffing agency recruiter or account manager will provide you their own email address and phone number; and you will have to communicate with the hiring manager through the staffing agent.

Understanding how technology and staffing agency services have evolved, I don't bother trying to send thank you notes to hiring managers after the interview if the staffing agent does not provide me the hiring manager's email address. This is an unwritten rule but acceptable practice when you do not have access to the hiring manager's contact information. If I'm provided the hiring manager's email address from the staffing agent, then I'll send the hiring manager a thank you note after the interview.

Perfecting Your Craft

There's no better time to perform a self-evaluation on your interview performance than right after you completed one. Ask yourself what you did well in the interview and what you need work on. Take this time to pat yourself on the back for the things you did well; and don't be so hard on yourself during your self-evaluation for the things you did wrong. You should be your greatest cheerleader whether your team is winning or losing the game.

Here are a few tips for perfecting your interviewing skills for your next job interview:

Tip #1: While the interview questions are still fresh in your mind, try to write down every question that was asked of you whether you knew the answer or not. By writing down these questions, and finding the correct answers to them, you have a better barometer of how well you performed in your technical and cultural fit for the job.

This will also give you valuable interview questions and answers that you can review for future interviews. There's a good chance these same questions may be asked in future job interviews. The one thing that started me on the road to writing this book was my habit of writing down the questions I was asked during job interviews.

Tip #2: Go over in your mind how you presented your introduction to your interviewer panel. Were you cool, calm and collected? Did you remember everything you wanted to say? Did you hit on all the right points that showed you were both a good technical fit as well as a good cultural fit to the company? Make note of the things you could have done better so you can remember to incorporate those corrections in future job interviews.

Tip #3: Evaluate how the effect of using role-playing, power poses, power thoughts and power words helped your confidence in your job interview. Did you remember to smile and maintain eye contact; hold your head up, shoulders back and chest out; and sit or stand upright in a relaxed and comfortable manner? Were there other things you could have done to make yourself feel more comfortable and confident on the phone or in the interview room? If so, make those adjustments in confidence boosting exercises for future job interviews.

Tip #4: How effective was your research on the company or interviewers? Did your research prove useful? Were you able to incorporate that information into the discussion, such as during your introduction? Did you strike a positive chord with any of your interviewers when talking about some of your personal interests, such as your hobbies, sports, volunteer work or other ways you spend your free time?

All of these things added to their perception of your cultural fit in their company. If any interviewers showed interest in your activities outside of work, you might want to consider using those same items in your next interview to establish your cultural fit and rapport with your interviewers.

Other Job Opportunities

Just because you are scheduled for a job interview, that's no reason to discontinue or place on hold your job search activities with other recruiters. I can't tell you how many times I thought the stars had aligned in my favor and I decided to forego pursuing other job opportunities that recruiters were offering me while I waited for the good news from the hiring manager after interviewing for the job. Then I realized those were shooting stars I was looking at because my hopes soon disappeared when I was notified that I was not selected for the job. By the time I tried to re-engage with those other recruiters I had put off, those jobs had already been filled.

Note to self: Stop stargazing after the job interview is over and keep pursuing other job opportunities that are out there. Until you sign your offer letter for the job, nothing is concrete about the outcome of your job interview.

Keep your job search pipeline open for other job opportunities that come your way even if you are scheduled for a job interview. There's nothing illegal or unprofessional about speaking with several recruiters about different job opportunities at the same time. You can be sure both those recruiters and employers are contacting several candidates at the same time, even if they currently have a scheduled interview with you.

If things don't work in your favor after your interview, hopefully you'll have several fallback recruiters you can turn to immediately. The quickest way to get over the post-interview blues is to be communicating with other staffing agency recruiters about other job opportunities.

If you are hired for the job after your interview, you can proudly announce to the other recruiters you were communicating with that you are no longer looking for work.

The Wait and the Response

How long you have to wait after your job interview before you receive a response or feedback depends on the hiring manager or the staffing agency's recruiter or account manager.

If the interviewing panel rated you as a potential fit for their team after your interview, and they still have other candidates to interview, the hiring manager will wait until his interview panel has completed all other interviews before making a decision on which candidate is the best fit for his team. This process could take 1–3 weeks depending on how many candidates are being interviewed and where you are in the interview pecking order.

After all candidates are interviewed, the hiring manager will let your staffing agency recruiter or account manager know if they selected you or not. If you did not use a staffing agency and worked directly with the employer's HR rep, the HR rep will email or call you to inform you of either the good news that you were selected or the bad news that you were passed over by the hiring manager.

What Happens If the Answer is No

If your interview performance convinced the hiring manager and his panel that you are not the best fit for their team, the hiring manager will pass this feedback immediately to the staffing agency recruiter or account manager that set up your interview with the employer. The hiring manager will not wait until all interviews are completed to pass along this bad news to the staffing agency. The manager will let the staffing agency do the dirty work of informing you that you were not selected. If your interview was set up through the employer's HR department instead of through a staffing agency, the HR rep will let you know that you were not selected for this job.

Whether the results about your job interview turn out positive or negative, always show some class and be a professional by thanking the people who made your interview possible—your staffing agents and the hiring manager. If the staffing agent is giving you the news over the phone, thank them there on the spot; otherwise an email to the agent will suffice. As previously mentioned in the section on sending a thank you note, you may not have access to the hiring manager's email address. In this case, you can opt to pass on your appreciation to the hiring manager through the staffing agency if you so desire.

Some staffing agencies will not contact you after the hiring manager has informed them that they did not select you for the job.

You have two options when you've waited long enough for feedback about your job interview:

1. The first option is to reach out to your staffing agent for status.

2. The second option is to accept the staffing agent's silence as meaning the hiring manager has not selected you for the job.

The first option is the best option because there could be multiple unplanned reasons that could delay a response back to you. There could be an unexpected number of candidates submitted from various recruiters that the hiring manager wants to interview. The hiring manager or other key members of the interview panel may be out of office for personal or business reasons; so they're waiting for that person to return. One or more pressing company issues or priorities may have placed the job interview process on hold. The company may be undergoing critical changes, such as management, hiring manager or organizational changes, which require the dust to settle on this internal transition before they can refocus on the interview process again.

I've contacted staffing agents for feedback after a week or two of waiting, and oftentimes they've told me the delay was due to the reasons I just mentioned. So be easy on the recruiter. Don't pester the staffing agent or the hiring manager with multiple inquiries each week. Just one inquiry is needed. Maintain a courteous and professional attitude throughout this waiting period.

The second option is to accept the staffing agent's silence as meaning the hiring manager has not selected you for the job. I've used this option when I know I absolutely bombed my job interview. I could not answer the majority of the questions, so I already knew I was not a good technical fit for that job. Under these circumstances, if I chose to contact the staffing agent, it would only be to confirm what the staffing agent and I already knew—I was not selected for the job.

Regardless of the choice you make to learn about your interview results; if it ends up being you were not selected for the job, move on and continue your job search with other staffing agents. Has this happened to me after a job interview? Yes, many times.

How to Handle Rejection after a Job Interview

Rejection is a normal part of the job search process just as in other areas of life. Everyone has to go through it from candidates running for the US presidential office to candidates in search of work in the most menial of jobs. Don't let the rejection from a failed job interview or the silence from recruiters hamstring or derail your momentum, enthusiasm, progress and success in your job search process.

Some people have a hard time with rejection. It makes them feel like a failure. They mistakenly identify an event with who they are as a person. It's not your failures that define you; it's how you respond to failures that matters. Failures refine you; they don't define who you are. You are not a failure just because you didn't get selected after a job interview. You are a successful person who experienced a failure. There's a difference.

Accept failures in life as a good teacher; the way you would accept the scores and remarks your teachers gave you on your paper in school. They are there to help improve your skills in life. Learn from failures the way you would learn from a coach telling you what you're doing wrong so you can improve your skills and performance to do better next time. They are there to make you a success, a winner, a champion in life. Embrace failures the way you did when you first embraced learning to ride a bike or skates or skateboard or snowboard or skis. Falling was all part of the process to rising higher. It is part of the adventure, the risk, the excitement and the fun of learning how to do something well in life. Sure there will be some bumps and bruises along the way when you fall, but when you get back up and move on with your life, you become stronger, better and wiser for having gone through those falls.

Both players and coaches in professional sports know this mentor, teacher and life coach called *failure* all too well. Each year, these professional athletes and coaches fail to win games and are rejected, traded or fired from teams only to find themselves being hired again by another team, performing better and winning games another year. That's what failure produces—***SUCCESS***!

201

Failure is the secret ingredient to the recipe of success.

During Neo's early developing stages in *The Matrix* film, his trainer Morpheus orders Tank the Operator to load the jump program for Neo. The whole crew of the Nebuchadnezzar hovercraft is watching with anticipation and bated breath to see how Neo will fare during his first-time jump from one rooftop to the next. Most of the crew members are convinced that ***everyone***, including Neo, ***falls the first time***.

As you prepare to jump from one job to the next; remember, everyone falls every now and then. Every great champion has experienced failure and defeat. The key to success is getting back up and trying again.

LeBron James has won three NBA championships; received four NBA MVP Awards, three NBA Finals MVP Awards, two Olympic gold medals; in addition to being selected to 12 NBA All-Star teams, 12 All-NBA teams and six All-Defensive teams. In 2016, LeBron was the key reason the Cleveland Cavaliers won their first NBA Finals championship in franchise history. So what's LeBron's view on failure? He said, *"You have to be able to accept failure to get better . . . You can't be afraid to fail. It's the only way you succeed—you're not gonna succeed all the time, and I know that."*

Theodor Roosevelt, the 26th US President, said, *"Far better is it to dare mighty things, to win glorious triumphs, even though checkered by failure . . . than to rank with those poor spirits who neither enjoy nor suffer much, because they live in a gray twilight that knows not victory nor defeat."*

H. Stanley Judd, author, film producer, communications consultant and president of The Executive Golfer and Golf School Online said, *"Don't waste energy trying to cover up failure. Learn from your failures and go on to the next challenge. It's OK to fail. If you're not failing, you're not growing."*

Vince Lombardi, the man the National Football League's Super Bowl trophy is named after, is best known as head coach of the Green Bay Packers during the 1960s where he led his team to three straight and five total NFL championships in seven years including winning the first two Super Bowls following the 1966 and 1967 NFL seasons. Lombardi is considered by many to be one of the best and most successful coaches in NFL history. He said, *"The greatest accomplishment is not in never falling, but in rising again after you fall."*

Abraham Lincoln, the 16th US President, said, *"My great concern is not whether you have failed, but whether you are content with your failure."*

Colin Powell, former US Secretary of State and retired four-star general in the US Army said, *"Success is the result of perfection, hard work, learning from failure, loyalty, and persistence."*

Zig Ziglar, motivational speaker, salesman and author with 10 of his 28 books on the best-seller lists whose books have been translated into more than 38 languages and dialects said, *"Remember that failure is an event, not a person . . . If you learn from defeat, you haven't really lost."*

Michael Jordan led the Chicago Bulls to two separate NBA championship "three-peats" in 1991, 1992, 1993 and again in 1996, 1997, 1998 after coming out of a two-year retirement in 1993 and 1994. He set an NBA record with 72 regular-season wins in the 1995-96 NBA season. Jordan said, *"I've missed more than 9,000 shots in my career. I've lost almost 300 games. Twenty-six times, I've been trusted to take the game winning shot and missed. I've failed over and over and over again in my life. And that is why I succeed . . . I can accept failure, everyone fails at something. But I can't accept not trying."*

Woody Allen is a well-known comic, producer, entertainer, director, Oscar-winner and screen star whose career spans more than 50 years. He won four Academy Awards and has more screenwriting Academy Award nominations than any other writer. Allen said, *"If you're not failing every now and again, it's a sign you're not doing anything very innovative."*

Denis Waitley is a graduate of the US Naval Academy at Annapolis, motivational speaker and writer. He said, *"Failure should be our teacher, not our undertaker. Failure is delay, not defeat. It is a temporary detour, not a dead end. Failure is something we can avoid only by saying nothing, doing nothing, and being nothing."*

J. K. Rowling is the British novelist best known for writing the *Harry Potter* fantasy series whose writings became blockbuster films and theme parks. Rowling said, *"It is impossible to live without failing at something, unless you live so cautiously that you might as well not have lived at all, in which case you have failed by default."*

Benjamin Franklin's face graces our $100 bill. He was a politician, author, printer, postmaster, civic activist, scientist and inventor. Franklin was one of the Founding Fathers of the United States and the first US Ambassador to France. He invented the lightning rod and provided a better understanding of electricity through his famous experiment of flying a kite in lightning. He also invented bifocals and the Franklin stove that was an improvement over fireplaces during his era. Franklin said in response to his many failed experiments, *"I didn't fail the test; I just found 100 ways to do it wrong."*

Steve Jobs was co-founder and CEO of Apple, CEO of Pixar Animation Studios and NeXT Inc., and on the board of directors of The Walt Disney Company. He was fired from Apple in 1985. Afterward, he founded the company NeXT and helped in the creation of Pixar that produced the first fully computer-animated film, *Toy Story*. Concerning his being fired by Apple, Steve Jobs responded with these words: *"I didn't see it then, but it turned out that getting fired from Apple was the best thing that could have ever happened to me. The heaviness of being successful was replaced by the lightness of being a beginner again, less* *sure about everything. It freed me to enter one of the most creative periods of my life.*"

John Elway is the executive vice president of football operations/General Manager for the Denver Broncos. After losing 43-8 to the Seattle Seahawks in Super Bowl XLVIII (48) in 2014, Mr. Elway said, "*We will use this as an experience that we went through, be disappointed that we didn't play better, but the bottom line is this organization and what (team owner) Pat Bowlen wants from this organization—that has not changed and it will not change. The bottom line is we're going to work as hard as we worked this year, if not harder, and continue to do that with the mindset that we want to be world champions and we're going to do everything we can to get there.*"

Congratulations to the 2016 Denver Broncos Super Bowl 50 champions!

If you failed one of your job interviews; were passed over by the hiring manager for another candidate; consider yourself in good company. People greater than you have fallen a lot farther and harder than you; but they got back up and tried again.

That's what made them great!

That's what made them successful!

That's what made them a champion!

Let your failures teach you; let them refine you; let them improve you; but never let them stop you. Now get back up and try again. There is greatness in you. You are destined for success. **You're a champion!**

Straight From My Heart

I wrote this book to give you help, wisdom, encouragement, confidence and success in your job interviews. It is my sincere hope that this book has blessed you, inspired you, strengthened and encouraged you.

I gain no greater satisfaction in life than to pass along to others the things I've learned to help you live a successful, healthy and prosperous life—not just in this life but the next. What do I mean by the *next life*?

The last and most important interview questions: I'm not saying this will happen anytime soon, but if you were to die today, where would you go? If God were to ask you why should He let you into heaven, what would you say?

Here's your answer: The Bible says in Romans 3:23, *"We've all sinned and fallen short of God's glory."* Romans 6:23 says, *"The wages of sin is death and separation from God, but the free gift of God is eternal life and peace from God."* (see also Isaiah 59:2 and Romans 5:1) Romans 10:9 says, *"If you confess with your mouth the Lord Jesus and believe in your heart that God raised Jesus from the dead, you shall be saved."* Romans 10:13 says, *"Whoever calls on the name of the Lord Jesus shall be saved."*

Pray this quick prayer with me: *Heavenly Father, I believe Jesus died on the cross for me and my sins, and rose again from the dead. I give You my life. Lord Jesus, come into my heart and into my life. Amen.*

If you prayed that prayer, you are saved and going to heaven when you die because Jesus paid for all your sins—past, present and future sins. That's your answer to your final and most important interview question of why God should let you into heaven.

ALSO BY FRANK McCLAIN

Did you like the *YOU'RE HIRED!* book? Then you'll enjoy my multi-award-winning book ***Job Hunting Ninja Master 2017*.**

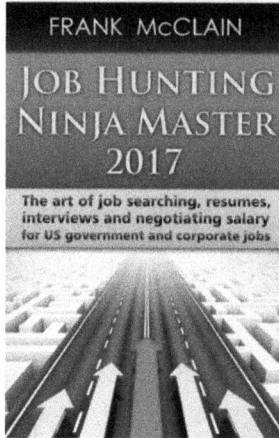

IT Questions & Answers For IT Job Interviews, Volume 1
IT Questions & Answers For IT Job Interviews, Volume 2
IT Questions & Answers For IT Job Interviews, Volume 3
IT Questions & Answers For IT Job Interviews, Volume 4
IT Questions & Answers For IT Job Interviews, Volume 5
IT Questions & Answers For IT Job Interviews, Volume 6

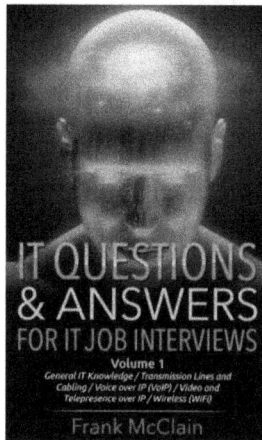

Did the *YOU'RE HIRED!* book help you? Then please do me this huge favor and write a book review on the Amazon website for this book at http://amzn.to/2sjygZy. This Amazon link will take you to this book's page; then go to the bottom of the page and click the "**Write a customer review**" button. It's that simple. As an indie author seeking customer reviews for my book, I greatly appreciate and value your review—*Thank you*!

Give this book as a gift to a friend or family member as an eBook or paperback.

If this book helped you, inspired you or gave you a better understanding of the interview process, tell your connected friends about this book on social media. It's a great way to let your friends know about a great book that will help both you and them; and your friends will thank you for it. Let me be one of the first to say *THANK YOU* for introducing your friends to a book that will change their careers and their lives for the better.

One Last Thing . . .

Be the first to find out when the next books I'm writing will come out by signing up on my email list at this link: http://bit.ly/2ffZcmx. I will not sell your email to marketers nor contact you for any other reason than to let you know when my next books are out on the market. When you sign up, you'll receive a confirmation email from "**Frank McClain confirmations@madmimi.com**"; so check your spam inbox if you don't see this confirmation email in your Inbox. It's that simple.

Frank McClain

About The Author

Frank McClain is a multi-award-winning author who graduated with a BS in Information Systems Management from the University of Maryland. He is a military veteran who served 20 years in the US Air Force both in the US and Europe. He lived and worked in Europe for over 12 years both as a US military member and as a civilian government contractor. He's worked over 15 years as an IT consultant in both US government and corporate jobs in the US and Europe. Frank has extensive experience dealing with the job search process, job recruiters, interviewing for jobs and working for many Fortune 500 companies and US government agencies, such as the North American Aerospace Defense Command (NORAD), Missile Defense Agency (MDA) and the Defense Information Systems Agency (DISA). Frank currently resides in Colorado.

www.ingramcontent.com/pod-product-compliance
Lightning Source LLC
Chambersburg PA
CBHW070953040426
42443CB00007B/491